"Michele Howe is an author \
drawing us to step closer to ~~~~~ ~~~~~~ ~~~~, ...~
ing Freedom and Joy in Self-Forgetfulness, contains short chapters that
explain how important it can be to balance self-focus with focusing on
others and God. It includes good practical tools to apply. In such perilous
and uncertain times, this is the perfect book to read and 'put feet to.' "

—**Robyn Besemann, Robyn B Ministries, Author**
Chained No More **small group studies**

"This book introduced a new concept to me: self-forgetfulness. I minister
to single parents and the divorced. Self-forgetfulness is a fresh concept for
my friends who have many divorce crises facing them daily. I shared with
my DivorceCare group about self-forgetfulness and not concentrating on
all the crisis in our lives and in our world but allowing our souls to com-
mune with the Lord as we forget self. Michele has done a wonderful job
on this book, the stories and especially the scriptures. Self-forgetfulness
is the path to joyful inner freedom."

—**Linda Ranson Jacobs, Author**
The Single Parent Confident and Successful

"Michele Howe has done it again! She's taken a hugely important topic I
had never even thought of and helped me understand why it matters in
my life—and does so in her usual fearless yet compassionate manner. If
you've never read any of Howe's books before, this is a great one to start
with. If you are already a fan, then you're in for a treat!"

—**Rick Johnson, Best-selling Author**
Becoming Your Spouse's Better Half **and**
How to Talk So Your Husband Will Listen

"If you need to know how to move forward from the anxieties, uncertainties, and unclear times we live in, read this book. In it, Michele Howe
gives practical action steps and biblical advice that will restore your joy
and renew your faith. Don't miss this outstanding book!"

—**Carol Kent, Speaker and Author**
He Holds My Hand: Experiencing God's Presence and Protection

"Michele shares incredibly powerful truth that leads to a peaceful, joy-filled life. I realized as I read that I was nodding emphatically, agreeing with her wise words. 'Trusting God + Self-forgetfulness = Joyful Inner Freedom.' Absolutely! Read the book and apply it. It will be life-changing."

—**Keri Kitchen, MEd, LPCC, NCC**
Faith and Focus Coach
Host of *The Every Day Royalty* Podcast

"In a culture riddled with self-obsession, Michele Howe brings us a refreshing new outlook. In *Finding Freedom and Joy in Self-Forgetfulness*, Michele encourages us to take our eyes off of ourselves and turn them toward our heavenly Father. This is where our journey to true freedom and authentic self-worth begins—by looking upward, not inward! Michele's book invites us to live a positive and productive life as we shift our focus from self to a deeper relationship with the One who created us. I know you will be strengthened in both your relationships and your life."

—**Karol Ladd, Best-selling Author**
The Power of a Positive Woman

"In unprecedented times of crisis and fear, author Michele Howe provides a solid path through anxiety, irritability, and sleeplessness. If you are overwhelmed by the unknowns, *Finding Freedom and Joy in Self-Forgetfulness* will help you exchange worry for stability, and turn uncertainty into an opportunity to reach out and serve others within your community. This present hour is the perfect time to trust in the Lord and do good."

—**PeggySue Wells, Founder of SingleMomCircle.com**
Best-selling author of 29 books, including
The Ten Best Decisions a Single Mom Can Make

"*Finding Freedom and Joy in Self-Forgetfulness* will keep you looking up to the Father. Jesus came to give us abundant life and set us free. This book will guide the way for you to experience living in freedom *daily* and offer you encouragement."

—**Lucille Williams, Author**
From Me to We: The Intimacy You Crave

"In *Finding Freedom and Joy in Self-Forgetfulness*, Michele offers a powerfully insightful book filled with wisdom and confidence to live the Christian life with joy. In her book on living life in the way of servanthood, Michele introduces the concept of self-forgetfulness, which helps us grasp how to train ourselves to shift the focus from our desires to serve others. She combines stories of everyday situations with the truth of Scripture to explore how self-forgetfulness leads to a life of freedom and joy. The call to finding joyful freedom in self-forgetfulness at the end of each chapter was both encouraging and challenging to me.

"Each chapter is filled with reassurance of God's faithfulness and how positioning our hearts in self-forgetfulness allows us to serve him and others better. The chapter on prayer was especially powerful to me: 'When we adopt the perspective that God calls us to not "simply bear up under adversity" in prayer, but to "persevere (to press forward) in the face of it," then we move into the dynamic, active realm of praying with self-forgetfulness.' We can often overlook the power of prayer, but this chapter is a great reminder of how our perseverance and servant hearts will build the trust we need in God's perfect answers in his timing."

—Rayna Neises, Speaker and Certified Coach
Author of *No Regrets: Hope for Your Caregiving Season*

"Author Michele Howe has done it again: she has delivered a personally relevant book guaranteed to challenge our way of thinking. The biblical concepts in this book encourage us to live a sacrificial life that leads to joy from the inside out. *Finding Freedom and Joy in Self-Forgetfulness* shows us the way to deny self as we follow Christ and serve others. Each chapter identifies a different challenge or opportunity to shape our minds and hearts into the image of Christ. What do I like most? I can't decide if it's the real-life stories she shares, the prayers, or the action steps toward change."

—Kathy Carlton Willis, Speaker and Author of
***The Grin Gal's Guide to Joy* and**
The Grin Gal's Guide to Well-Being

FINDING FREEDOM
AND JOY IN
Self-Forgetfulness

MICHELE HOWE

FINDING
FREEDOM
AND JOY IN
Self-Forgetfulness

HENDRICKSON
PUBLISHERS

an imprint of Hendrickson Publishing Group

Finding Freedom and Joy in Self-Forgetfulness

© 2021 Michele Howe

Published by Hendrickson Publishers
an imprint of Hendrickson Publishing Group
Hendrickson Publishers, LLC
P. O. Box 3473
Peabody, Massachusetts 01961-3473
www.hendricksonpublishinggroup.com

ISBN 978-1-68307-356-7

Printed in the United States of America

First Printing — November 2021

Library of Congress Control Number: 2021945498

To all my dear friends (near and far) who remind me to live a self-forgetful life. You demonstrate in beautiful ways how joyful freedom is set into motion once we take that first faith-driven step toward self-sacrificially loving others. Thank you for your godly examples and your fervent constancy in seeking to know Christ and make him known.

Contents

Acknowledgments   xiii

Introduction   1

1. Why Self-Forgetfulness?   3
2. The Link between Self-Forgetfulness and Joyful
   Inner Freedom   9
3. Growing from Self-Focused to Self-Forgetful   14
4. Being Mindful of Living Peacefully Self-Forgetful   19
5. How to Start Living a Self-Forgetful Life   25
6. Why God Blesses the Self-Forgetful and Those
   Who Forgive   30
7. God Empowers Those Who Live to Serve   36
8. Self-Forgetfulness—In the Home   41
9. Self-Forgetfulness—In the Workplace   46
10. Self-Forgetfulness—In Our Churches   51
11. Self-Forgetfulness—In Our Neighborhoods   57
12. Self-Forgetfulness—With Our Families   62
13. Self-Forgetfulness—With Our Friends   67
14. Self-Forgetfulness—With Our Acquaintances   72
15. How Self-Forgetfulness Changes Us   77
16. How Self-Forgetfulness Matures Us   82

17. How Self-Forgetfulness Humbles Us   87
18. How Self-Forgetfulness Challenges Us   92
19. How Self-Forgetfulness Encourages Us   98
20. How Self-Forgetfulness Stretches Us to Serve   103
21. Taking Self-Forgetfulness into Our Prayer Rooms   108
22. Praying Big Self-Forgetful Prayers   113
23. Praying with Self-Forgetfulness for Eternal Purposes   118
24. How Self-Forgetfulness Changes the Way We
    View Our Weaknesses   123
25. How Self-Forgetfulness Changes the Way We Think   128
26. How Self-Forgetfulness Changes the Way We Speak   134
27. How Self-Forgetfulness Changes the Way We Listen   139
28. How Self-Forgetfulness Changes the Way We See
    People   144
29. How Self-Forgetfulness Changes the Way We
    Interpret the World   149
30. How Self-Forgetfulness Changes the Way We
    Worship God   154

Sources for Quotations   159

Acknowledgments

I've been humbled and blessed to live an author's dream by being privileged to write time and again for the same publishing house. Anyone who knows me well is aware that I treasure long-lasting, time-enduring relationships—both professional and personal. From my perspective, the more you invest in a person, a project, or a group of individuals, the richer the relationship, the end result, and the deeper the eternal impact upon one another. What's not to love? That said, I want to offer my sincerest thanks to everyone at the Hendrickson Publishing Group beginning with Paul Hendrickson, publisher, for catching the vision of how this book on self-forgetfulness will impact our world for Jesus Christ in a dynamic way.

To Patricia Anders, my editor extraordinaire, who is the editorial director at Hendrickson and without fail instinctively knows what words I'm grasping for and expertly edits my work so that you, dear reader, understand too. Thank you, Patricia. You amaze me with your stunning work on each and every book, and I'm ever so grateful for you and for the friendship we've developed over the years (through many book collaborations, despite the miles between us). You are a treasure to me both professional and personal.

I also want to give my warmest thanks to Dave Pietrantonio, Hendrickson's book production manager, who organizes all the behind-the-scenes production details and does so with apparent ease! To Meg Rusick, Sarah Welch, and Phil Frank. I'm so thankful for each of you, and I'm always excited to hold the finished product in my hand. I smile and think of you all and your fine contributions toward making that happen whenever a box arrives at my home with the Hendrickson logo printed on the sides.

Finally, my ongoing thanks to my agent at the Steve Laube Agency, Bob Hostetler. You are a good man to have in my corner, and I appreciate you more than you know.

To the many faithful readers of my twenty-six plus books spanning over twenty years now, thank you! I always think about the term "circle of life" as it relates to writing and reading. We authors catch an idea or see a need and the seed of a book is born in our hearts and minds. We present a proposal to a publisher and if accepted for publication, an entire team of individuals then contributes their finest skills to its creation. The finished product is then passed on to you, the reader, where you invest your time and attention to reading and absorbing the words found within these pages. Then readers pass on what they've read to others through selfless actions and uplifting words, spiritually revitalized to see God's kingdom spread to the four corners of our world. A single book's message can be boundless, and you, dear readers, are responsible for that eternal investment. Thank you for being part of sharing this vision of knowing Christ and making him known in the world!

Introduction

If there's ever been a time when I needed to pursue an intentional, self-forgetful life, it's now. Throughout the past year, I have wrestled more intensely than ever before with fully trusting God to meet my needs instead of trusting in my own strengths, strategies, and resources to provide for myself and those I love. I've often been reminded of the biblical account of Jacob when he went to sleep the night before meeting his estranged brother Esau and "wrestled" with God through those dark hours. By morning, Jacob had prevailed, but he sustained a permanent limp: a continual reminder of his constant need to rely on God.

I so relate to the emotional, mental, physical, and spiritual travail Jacob endured that night when he felt afraid of the many uncertainties that would affect him, his family, and the entire community that traveled with him. Although God didn't meet me in a dream as he did Jacob, I feel like I've spent much of this past year wrestling to fully rely on God so that I can self-forgetfully reach out and serve others in love. God has been doing a refining work in my own heart, and though it's been painful and hard daily death to self-reliance, I can say it has been for my good and his glory.

Now you know my personal reason for writing this new book, *Finding Freedom and Joy in Self-Forgetfulness*. As I was forced to stretch and grow these past months, I took note of others who were not merely surviving but thriving. Their secret? They, too, were learning the same lesson God was imparting to me: Self-forgetfulness is the path to joyful inner freedom. As you read the stories found in this book, you'll discover how this biblically robust Christian principle sets believers free from the inside out.

As disciples of Christ who seek to live hour-by-hour from a position of intentional self-forgetfulness, we can set into motion a beautiful display of God's grace in our lives that spills over into other lives in dramatic, life-enhancing ways. When we trust the Lord to care for our needs, and we entrust ourselves to his keeping, he empowers us to live more fearlessly and freely. Too often, believers become internally paralyzed, which keeps them from serving others with abandon, simply because they take God out of the equation.

My deepest hope and prayer is that as you read these stories, you too will find the paradoxical biblical principle of self-forgetfulness growing in your own life. As you seek to trust God with all your heart, soul, and spirit, he will meet your every need and equip you to reach out in selfless, self-sacrificial love to those people God places in your path. Ready to take that first faith-filled step? Let's go!

Chapter 1

Why Self-Forgetfulness?

Trust in the LORD and do good; dwell in the land and
enjoy safe pasture. Take delight in the LORD, and
he will give you the desires of your heart. Commit
your way to the LORD; trust in him and he will do
this: He will make your righteous reward shine like
the dawn, your vindication like the noonday sun. Be
still before the LORD and wait patiently for him.

Psalm 37:3–7

*All of us desperately need contentment, a state of inner
peace separate from our circumstances. Ultimately,
contentment is more a shift in attitude than a change in
circumstances. When difficult circumstances come into
my life, I hear God's voice saying, "Let Me be the Blessed
Controller. Surrender. Accept my timing. Accept my ways.
Accept my outcome. Let your trust be in Me alone."*

Linda Dillow

In early 2020, the rumblings of the COVID-19 pandemic began ramping up in the news with increased warnings and dire predictions of apocalyptic proportions. Wherever I went, the conversations turned—at least briefly—to what was happening throughout the world and how it would affect us in the United States. As a recovering perfectionist and professional planner, I started thinking, "Is this something I need to be paying closer attention to so that we're prepared for the worst?" Seeking to get ahead of what I thought might happen if people began to panic, I started considering all the resources my immediate family (and extended family) might need should we face shortages. The problem with spending so much time anticipating and planning for the worst is that I quickly began to feel overwhelmed by the unknowns. I became weary from trying to overthink the best next steps and irritable when my nearest and dearest didn't always agree with my perspective.

I soon realized I was consumed with trying to be in control of this crisis. And I wasn't alone. Friends, family, colleagues, and women within my community began expressing the very same emotions I had been dealing with since this crisis erupted. Fear. Uncertainty. Worry. Anxiety. Sleeplessness. Irritability. Lack of focus. You name it and someone within my immediate circle experienced it.

Taking a figurative (and literal) deep breath, I stepped away from the news reports, the updates, and the dire predictions to quiet my heart and mind before the Lord. I realized there were several things I needed to do in the center of this worldwide crisis—and stocking my pantry wasn't at the top of the list.

First, I silently waited before the Lord, in the quiet and all alone. I allowed his perfect peace to sweep over me like a cleansing flood and wash away all the pent-up anxiety and burdens. I meditated on verses that reminded me of God's perfect provision and promised protection. I asked for forgiveness for trying to take control and anticipate the needs of myself and my family, which made me forget God's promise to give me what I need *one day at a time.* No hoarding allowed.

Next, I prayed that in the coming days, weeks, and months, I would begin each day determined to be self-forgetful, ready to reach out and be used by God to meet the needs of others. So, I did just that. Every day, the global, national, state, and local news continues to blare the worst of the worst, and yet my heart is peaceful because I know God is still God.

Each morning, there have been fresh opportunities for me and my family to reach out and serve others within our community. I've been blessed, encouraged, and humbled by what I see God doing in the hearts of believers who trust him to meet their needs so that they're free to serve others. Never before have I been so convinced that as a Christ-follower, this present hour is the perfect time to forget about ourselves, trust that God knows what we each need, and reach out in sacrificial love to those he brings our way. For you and for me, our mantra should be, "Trust in the LORD and do good."

Self-forgetfulness is a powerful, eternity-motivated attitude of the heart that every believer needs to embrace. As I observe Christians from around the world respond to an unknown and seemingly uncontainable virus, it is clear that those who are purposeful in giving thanks (honing a humble, grateful heart) in these difficult days have an inner calm that others who rail against heaven (and the governing authorities) do not possess. Not only are these thankful individuals inwardly at peace, but they are also given to generous acts of self-sacrifice.

Self-forgetfulness not only does me good; it does the whole world good. When I'm confident that God is my provider, I'm far and away freer in every way imaginable to extend myself on another's behalf. It's only when I allow my heart to grow inwardly fearful about having to meet my every need in my own woefully inadequate strength and abilities that I become too paralyzed to do any good for those around me. When my confidence and trust are in the Lord and in him alone, only then can I step out and freely give to those people God brings along my path.

Happily, this freedom from self-focus is contagious. If you don't believe me, then consider how powerful a single act of kindness is and how our hearts soar whenever we witness it. As we look ahead into uncertain days, we can best prepare ourselves for whatever lies ahead by first knowing who God says he is and what he promises to do for his beloved children. Next, we thank him in advance for his perfect provision and pray that we're ready for service by learning to live life from a self-forgetful perspective. As we put into place these two synergic principles, we will experience a joyful freedom like we've never known. And that's a promise!

Take-away Action Thought

When I start to feel anxious and afraid, I will pore over those Scripture verses that declare God's promises to provide for my every need. I will memorize Philippians 4:19: "My God will meet all your needs."

6

My Heart's Cry to You, O Lord

Father, I find myself experiencing something I've never had to face before in this life. This worldwide panic and the outbreak of a virus have been terrifying. We have been and continue to be truly at your mercy. No matter what the world believes, I know you are my only source of hope, peace, and provision. You have promised to meet my every need. As I reflect on this wonderful and comforting truth, I am at peace. Help me to start each day in quiet reflection and prayer. Equip me to go out and be purposeful in forgetting about myself and my needs so I can serve those you bring into my life. I want to live each and every day in freedom, and I know that joyful freedom will come only when I put the full weight of my trust in you. Amen.

Finding Joyful Freedom in Self-Forgetfulness

1. Self-forgetfulness with others. "Trust in the LORD and do good." Awaken each day with an attitude of readiness to identify a need that I can meet. I will prayerfully ask the Lord to connect me to someone to whom I can be of practical service and encouragement.

2. Self-forgetfulness in me. "Commit your way to the LORD." Each day this week, I will spend time asking the Lord to reveal to me if there are areas of my life where I have not yet surrendered to his perfect plan and purpose. I will prayerfully reflect on recent attitudes, events, and circumstances and surrender to whatever God brings into my life, knowing it is for my good and his glory.

3. Self-forgetfulness with God. "Be still before the Lord and wait patiently for him." Every evening before I go to sleep, I will spend a designated time prayerfully revisiting my day. I will tell the Lord what I'm feeling and struggling with so that I'm keeping my lines of communication open with him. I'll close this end-of-day quiet time by reading a verse aloud so that my best and final thoughts before going to sleep are ones full of God's promised provision.

 *Chapter 2*

*The Link between Self-forgetfulness
and Joyful Inner Freedom*

"Surely I am with you always, to the very end of the age."
Matthew 28:20

*Jesus is with you today, tomorrow, and forever. He
is also ruling the whole universe and bringing
all things together for God's glory and your
good. You can trust him with your tomorrows.*
Edward Welch

We might very well create a mathematical equation for this biblical formula: *Trusting God + Self-forgetfulness = Joyful inner freedom.* It's that simple. Really. When I'm fully convinced that God will always be with me no matter what I face, then I am far more equipped, willing, and able to reach out toward you to meet your needs. Think about this: There is a direct relationship between the measure in which I trust God to meet my needs and my fearless willingness to step out in faith to meet yours. Not convinced? Then read on.

Some years ago, when my husband and I first received the news that his father had terminal cancer, we were shocked by the diagnosis. To add to that natural grief-stricken reaction, we also discovered that he had only a few months to live. As our minds started processing all the practical steps we would need to put into place for his ongoing treatments and personal care, we felt emotionally overwhelmed. We asked ourselves many questions. *How can we make the most of these brief short months together? How will we juggle all the medical related responsibilities? How will we handle our emotional highs and lows, grief, and sorrows of this long goodbye?*

To add further complications to this grief-filled scenario, our oldest daughter was preparing for her marriage. As she was the first of our children to marry, we all happily anticipated her wedding and were busy preparing for it.

We soon found our emotions volleying back and forth between grief and joy, even worrying that my father-in-law would pass away on our daughter's wedding day. Yes, we were caught in a very real struggle between celebrating one of life's most wonderful passages and walking through a transition to eternal life.

I remember crying out to the Lord for his sustaining strength, grace, and power. Through it all, of course, God was faithful to his word. One day at a time, he bestowed on us the strength and grace we needed for that day and hour. Realizing how easy it would have been for us to slip into feeling overwhelmed by sorrow during this hard season, I remember laying my head on my pillow every night and asking the Lord to give us a good night's sleep. And he did. During the daytime hours, we might wrestle through our shifting thoughts and emotions, yet God blessed us with rejuvenating sleep so that we were able to joyfully and freely serve others day after day.

Perhaps one of the most valuable lessons I learned during that season positioned between celebration and grief is that God was with us. He was always close by and sustaining us even when we felt we couldn't take another step. As we purposed in our hearts to serve my father-in-law as best as we could, while simultaneously preparing for our daughter's wedding, God blessed us with a joyful inner freedom born of hearts determined to serve others with self-forgetfulness. When I look back to that time, I am filled with humble gratitude, for we were able to truly celebrate our daughter's marriage, and six weeks later, we rejoiced that my father-in-law entered the presence of Jesus.

As we study the eternal truths found in God's word, we prepare ourselves to ably meet whatever he allows into our lives. Remember this: There is a reason why God desires us to spend time each day with him in the Scriptures. The daily renewing of our minds through Bible reading and study is precisely what he uses to help us think through and respond to life in a biblically robust way.

We never know what tomorrow may bring. We aren't even promised a tomorrow. Which is why I repeatedly tell others (and frequently remind myself) that today is the day I'm given to seek to know God more intimately. In this uncertain and dangerous world, how can we better equip ourselves for whatever may happen than by pouring over Scripture? How can you and I learn to trust a God we don't know very well? We can't.

Begin right now. Today. Commit yourself to daily Bible reading and prayer. Meditate throughout your day on a single verse from Scripture. Carry God's word with you wherever you go. Listen to Bible teaching when you drive, walk, or work around your home.

The link between self-forgetfulness and joyful inner freedom is attained only when we learn to trust God completely. Are you there yet? Have you started on this journey of deepening trust in our faithful heavenly Father? If not now, then when?

Take-away Action Thought

When I am tempted to despair because my emotions feel out of control, I will speak Jesus' words from Matthew 28:20 out loud and continue to meditate on them until my heart and mind are fully at rest.

My Heart's Cry to You, O Lord

Father, the circumstances of life are crowding in around me. I feel so many intense emotions, some good, and some that are very, very scary. I want to face these life situations fully confident that you are my sole provider of grace, strength, hope, and peace. You have promised to be with me always. And your word never lies. No matter how many challenges I may face today, I am purposing in my heart to trust you to meet my needs so that I can serve those around me with selfless abandon. Thank you, Lord, for your constancy of love, grace, and joy. Amen.

Finding Joyful Freedom in Self-Forgetfulness

1. Self-forgetfulness with others. "I am with you always." As I seek to selflessly serve those around me this week, I will faithfully remind others of Jesus' powerful promise. I will speak God's blessed, comforting truth into their lives so that they will know where to go in their own moments of desperation. I will give voice to the faith I have in Jesus Christ so that others might come to find that same eternal security I have.

2. Self-forgetfulness in me. "I am with you always." Each morning this week, I will prayerfully begin my day by meditating on this powerful truth. I will speak this promise to my heart so I can serve, give, and live with intentional self-forgetfulness throughout the day. And I will rest in the comforting knowledge that because the Lord walks with me, he will provide me with everything I need to carry out my service to him and others.

3. Self-forgetfulness with God. "I am with you always." Each evening this week, I will reflect on the Lord's faithfulness toward me that day. My prayers will reflect the spirit of joyful freedom I have discovered through walking by faith and letting go of my fears and worries.

Chapter 3

Growing from Self-Focused to Self-Forgetful

In repentance and rest is your salvation, in quietness and
trust is your strength. . . . The LORD longs to be gracious
to you; therefore he will rise up to show you compassion.

Isaiah 30:15, 18

*Faith in Jesus will not replace your fears. Instead, your faith
will coexist with your fears and begin to quiet them. You
will learn, by faith, to see your life from Jesus' perspective
and to trust that he is your ever-present help in trouble.*

Edward Welch

No one who was acquainted with Jen would have guessed
how intensely self-focused she was when she was alone.
To everyone who knew her, she was the most selfless
person they had ever met. In a way, this was true. Jen did her
best to live each day with a self-forgetful attitude, and she
succeeded—as far as it went on the outside. On the inside,
however, she fought a mental battle that could be relentless.

Jen got up each morning determined to be the best second-
grade teacher she could be. She prayed for wisdom and understanding to reach deeply into the hearts of those under her

care from 8:30 am to 3:00 pm each weekday. She even kept a prayer list that included the names of her second graders, and she prayed through this list daily, bringing the needs of these beloved youngsters before the throne of grace. Throughout the day, she focused on the physical, mental, and spiritual needs of her second-grade class. When the last bell rang for the day, she said her goodbyes, finished organizing her classroom, and then headed home. On her way home, Jen replayed her school-day conversations, making mental notes of any potential issues or problems she had become aware of in the lives of her students and their families. She even prayed a prayer of benediction of sorts for the day before pulling into her garage and shutting the door.

Typically, Jen unwound by changing into her comfortable walking clothes, opening her mail, and beginning her meal preparations. No matter the weather, she found it best to get outside and walk several miles around her neighborhood before settling in for the evening. She knew herself well. As soon as she finished her supper and cleaned her kitchen, she started thinking. Overthinking, to be more accurate. As a single woman who desired to marry and have a family of her own, she almost always began going down that familiar and mentally debilitating path of "what ifs." She struggled with private fears about growing old alone, without ever having her own husband and children to live life with. She frequently felt afraid of her own future.

Jen also experienced no small measure of guilt when she inwardly became so consumed about an unknown future that she would forget the multitude of God's daily blessings in her life that day. Her heart felt torn between resting in God's promised provision and wrestling with an unknown future. But Jen was learning something important. She was slowly making peace with the fact that her faith could coexist with her fears and even begin to quiet them. What an amazing truth! Slowly, she accepted that though she might continue to struggle with her fears, she gained spiritual strength each time she talked to Jesus about them and allowed him to quiet her fears with his ever-present love and help.

Can you relate? I sure can. Though the specifics of my own "what if?" worries differ from Jen's, I have the same habit of attempting to cope with all of life's possibilities without God. And that's never a good thing. It doesn't matter if my fears are of the large or small variety—when I remove God from the equation, I can't live the faith-filled, self-forgetful life that God desires for me. And neither can you.

This journey toward self-forgetfulness takes time and intentionality. It also requires taking God at his word and believing he will do what he has promised. If we are to live increasingly self-forgetful lives, we must become more and more intimately acquainted with the biblical principles for getting us there. I love how Jen made the connection between experiencing fears and then taking each one to Jesus in prayer so that he could quiet every single fear in his love.

Jesus wants us to learn that even though we may struggle with fears and worries throughout the day, he is eager to tenderly quiet each and every one. We will be tempted to lose ourselves in the midst of our fears, and our faith may struggle as we face very real hardships and suffering, but Jesus' perfect love toward us is always enough. Each time we turn toward him, acknowledging our fears and trusting him to work on our behalf, we add another page of God's faithfulness to the story of our personal faith journeys. And that, my friend, is a lesson we all can cherish.

Take-away Action Thought

When my heart begins to race and I start to replay my personal "what if?" fear-driven thoughts, I will immediately turn to Jesus and talk to him about what I'm worried about. I'll read and then meditate on this comforting truth found in Isaiah 30.

My Heart's Cry to You, O Lord

Father, please help me accept that my fears and my faith may coexist. Remind me that though the battle with my fears may never completely go away, I can learn to talk with you as soon as I begin to feel afraid. Help me to rest in your perfect love and provision for me. You know me better than I know myself. I am one of your beloved children. Give me the grace to rest in your plan for my life. I want to fully trust in your provision for me so that I can faithfully pour out my gifts and talents to those you have placed into my life. Amen.

Finding Joyful Freedom in Self-Forgetfulness

1. Self-forgetfulness with others. "In repentance and rest is your salvation." This week, I will be on the lookout for opportunities to share with others what God has done in my life.

2. Self-forgetfulness in me. "In quietness and trust is your strength." Anytime I begin to entertain those "what if?" questions about my life and future, I will stop myself.

Instead, I will read and then meditate on the comforting truth found in Isaiah 30. I'll exhale all my fears and worries and place them into God's hands.

3. Self-forgetfulness with God. "The LORD longs to be gracious to you." Before I go to sleep each night, I'll spend a few moments making note of God's perfect provision that took care of me that day. I'll then give thanks to God for each gracious act bestowed and tell others about them too.

Chapter 4

Being Mindful of Living Peacefully Self-Forgetful

You will keep in perfect peace those whose minds are steadfast, because they trust in you. Trust in the LORD forever, for the LORD, the LORD himself, is the Rock eternal.

Isaiah 26:3–4

Real, sturdy, lasting peace, peace that doesn't rise and fall with circumstances, isn't to be found in picking apart your life until you have understood all of the components. You will never understand it all because God, for your good and his glory, keeps some of it shrouded in mystery.

Paul David Tripp

Brad punched his timecard and jogged toward the parking lot. If he was able to leave the company's parking area before the mass exodus started, then he might arrive early today. The last thing he needed was to be even a few minutes late picking up his two sons from their after-school program. Ever since his ex-wife Lindsay divorced him the previous year, there had been an ongoing battle between them about anything and everything. Brad did his best to not give her an excuse to erupt in anger.

As he got into his car, he remembered for the umpteenth time how utterly blindsided he had been by the divorce papers Lindsay had cruelly delivered to his place of employment. It was devastating. Brad had no idea she was contemplating a permanent separation. But once the papers were signed, he had tried to deal with it in a manner that would honor God. He reminisced about how he and Lindsay had attended church together only a few years earlier. They served side-by-side in the children's ministry and, at Lindsay's urging, even hosted a weekly small group with mutual friends for dinner and Bible study. A few years into their marriage, they had two children of their own.

Then, without warning, Lindsay started to make excuses about missing Sunday services. She complained that she was too tired from work and caring for the boys. She then stopped serving in the children's ministry, saying she no longer had the energy for that either. Finally, she begged off hosting their small group too. Brad tried to understand what was happening inside of her heart and mind, but she became more distant with him by the day. Brad set up biblical counseling appointments, but she wasn't interested. After a while, he began going alone as he tried to sort out the ominous changes transpiring in his wife and in their marriage.

All hope Brad had of rebuilding their former faith-centered life came crashing down after he opened up the divorce papers. He felt like he was in the Twilight Zone. Nothing made any sense. But his confusion and personal pain didn't stop Lindsay from proceeding swiftly with the divorce. He prayed that once the legalities were complete, he and Lindsay might regain some of their former cordiality for the sake of co-parenting their two boys. But that wasn't to happen.

From one day to the next, Lindsay seemed strangely bent on punishing Brad via nasty texts, emails, and voicemails—thus his heightened awareness to do everything within his power to abide by the custody agreements to the letter so that Lindsay would have no reason to react angrily to him.

Exiting the parking lot in a timelier fashion than anticipated, Brad turned onto the street and began to pray aloud. "Lord, my life and my times are in your hands. Please help me to make it to the school on time. But even if I don't, Lord, help me to keep my mind on you. Give me peace in this impossible situation. I have my sons to think about now, and they need all the love I can give them. I'm counting on your grace and strength to be the dad I need to be. Amen."

Brad's mind was certainly full—of both the bitter and the sweet memories of his marriage before the divorce. Thankfully, his faith in God carried him through all the pain, uncertainty, and confusion. He wisely talked to God about everything he was facing and then allowed God's promises to speak peace into his hurting heart. As grief-filled and difficult as Brad's circumstances were, he was fully convinced that God was willing and able to supply him with what he needed to live each day full of peace, full of joy, and fully equipped to take on the new role of single dad to his boys. Brad's focus on God allowed him to live self-forgetfully so that he could bless his sons' lives to the fullest.

The question we ought to be asking ourselves as we try to be mindful is this: What do we choose to fill our minds with? Given that each of us will face situations, people, and circumstances that may provoke our emotions to rise and fall, we must be intentional with what we think about. Will we choose to make our default thinking centered on the truth found in God's word? Or will we lose ourselves in the emotional mire of defeat, depression, and discouragement? It really does come down to one intentional thought at a time. Either we will mindfully bow our hearts and minds before the throne of God and beseech him for the supernatural enablement to keep going despite what is happening all around us, or we will fall victim to the always-unpredictable, always-changing circumstances in life.

The sooner we learn to take our wandering thoughts captive and bring every one under subjection to Christ, the easier it will be for our minds to stay focused on God and his promises. Being mindful so that we can live self-forgetfully is essential to viewing life through Jesus' eternal perspective. Will we necessarily understand everything that happens? No, each of us will face questions that may only be answered in eternity. Because, as Paul Tripp so wisely points out, "God, for your good and his glory, keeps some of it shrouded in mystery."

Take-away Action Thought

When my mind starts to fixate on depressing, defeating, or discouraging thoughts, I will turn my attention to this promise in Isaiah 26 and begin saying it slowly out loud. I will prayerfully continue repeating its comforting truth until my faith is securely centered on what God can do for me, rather than what I am able to control and change.

My Heart's Cry to You, O Lord

Father, I found myself fighting a familiar mental battle again today. It started when a painful memory came to mind and I allowed myself to spend too much time revisiting all the heartbreak surrounding it. I felt angry, upset, and depressed. Lord, please help me to turn my thoughts back to you more quickly the next time this happens. Thank you for your always-faithful presence in my life. Thank you for your infallible word that directs my thoughts to you and your promised provision. Amen.

Finding Joyful Freedom in Self-Forgetfulness

1. Self-forgetfulness with others. "You will keep in perfect peace those whose minds are steadfast." I will begin each day this week prayerfully planning specific ways to encourage and bless those around me. I'll make a daily plan to interact and lift up each of these individuals according to their needs, and I'll encourage them to face their own challenges by keeping their focus on you at all times.

2. Self-forgetfulness in me. "[I] trust in you." Each evening this week, I will take a few moments to consider the challenging seasons in my life when I was forced to throw myself on God's mercy to get through the trials I was facing. I will purpose to become a good rememberer and an even more thankful Christ-follower, knowing that as I revisit the Lord's past supernatural deliverances, my faith will deepen and my peace will expand.

3. Self-forgetfulness with God. "The LORD himself is the Rock eternal." Using a Bible concordance and dictionary, I will study the biblical accounts where God is described as our Rock, so that I can widen my grasp of what this promise means in my life.

Chapter 5

How to Start Living a Self-Forgetful Life

For the grace of God has appeared that offers salvation
to all people. It teaches us to say "No" to ungodliness
and worldly passions, and to live self-controlled, upright
and godly lives in this present age, while we wait for the
blessed hope—that appearing of the glory of our great
God and Savior, Jesus Christ, who gave himself for us to
redeem us from all wickedness and to purify for himself a
people that are his very own, eager to do what is good.

Titus 2:11–14

*God is a giver of grace, the most powerful weapon in the
war for the heart. God's grace gives us power to say no to
powerful desires. It enables us to turn from the creation
toward the Creator. It makes us willing to forsake our
kingdoms for his. God's grace forgives, but it also constrains
and draws and wins. It is jealous, God-focused grace, fitted
for the moments we are tempted to follow our desires.*

Paul David Tripp

L iving in an old farmhouse for over thirty years has taught me one lesson in particular: something always needs fixing. From the day we moved into this family homestead, portions of which are over a hundred years old, my husband Jim and I recognized we had a job of major proportions staring us in the face. Season by season, year after year, we have fixed, upgraded, remodeled, torn out, and discarded the broken, battered, worn-out, no longer useful parts of our beloved home. Why, some might ask, would we go to so much bother and work? Because we value our home and want it to be in the best shape possible so that we can get the most use out of it, season by season and year after year.

Recently, Jim was placing new support beams in our basement after he removed and repainted the trim around our kitchen and before he updated some plumbing work. As I was working around him (and the mess), I thought about how our efforts to remake this old house into something sturdy, stable, and useful is like our intentionality to grow, mature, and become godlier in our spiritual walk. Think about it: We study, dissect, rebuild, and reassemble our houses, both literal and spiritual, all the time.

Because we have this blessed hope living within us, and because we desire to be purified from all wickedness so that we can do good in Jesus' name, we must start with the foundation of our heart's desires. Just as we continue to shore up our house's literal foundation so that it's safe, strong, and functional, we do the same in our spiritual lives. This blessed self-forgetful life begins with a repentant heart and a forgiven soul.

26

Preparing the heart's foundation is the first step to living a self-forgetful life. We must first come before the Lord in humble submission and confess that we can do nothing good in our own strength. We then acknowledge that the Holy Spirit working within us will equip us for all good works. So, the starting point for all spiritual change begins here. We confess we are sinners needing a Savior. We then repent (meaning we turn away from our sin and toward Christ), which allows us to begin our journey toward self-forgetfulness.

God's word tells us that he loves us so much that his eternally perfect love can also be described as a jealous love. When we allow idols to exist in our hearts and lives (anything we love more dearly than we love God), his perfect, jealous love for us begins to purify our hearts and minds. The Holy Spirit within us nudges us away from sinfulness and self-centered choices in favor of self-forgetfulness. This learning to live a self-forgetful life is not a journey of specific steps from start to finish. Rather, it's a lifelong, day-by-day, moment-by-moment, God-focused work of sanctification. In the same way that our farmhouse renovation projects are ongoing, the Holy Spirit is continually doing an internal work of heart purification in us. In sum, we start living a life of self-forgetfulness the moment we become God's children.

Take-away Action Thought

Whenever I begin to feel discouraged because of my lack of progress in learning to live intentionally self-forgetful, I will recite these verses from Titus 2:11–14 as a reminder that the Holy Spirit is always doing a fresh (and continuing) work of inner sanctification in my heart and mind.

My Heart's Cry to You, O Lord

Father, I am feeling discouraged about my lack of spiritual growth. Although I have every intention of living for others and forgetting about myself, I find I'm often not very successful. I struggle with my own heart idols and those desires that war against my spirit. Please help me to rely on your strength and grace and be comforted by the knowledge that you will never stop this work of sanctification in me. I long to be like Jesus in every way possible, but my flesh battles with this desire. Help me, Lord, to lean wholly on you and to trust in your faithfulness as you continue to purify and mature me from the inside out. Amen.

Finding Joyful Freedom in Self-forgetfulness

1. Self-forgetfulness with others. "The grace of God . . . offers salvation to all people." Early in the week, I'll compile a list of those individuals in my life who don't yet have a personal relationship with Christ. Each day, I will spend time praying for each person, asking the Lord to create seeking hearts within them. I will look for opportunities to gently share my own story of repentance and faith with them as God leads and allows.

2. Self-forgetfulness in me. "It teaches us to . . . live self-controlled, upright and godly lives." Each evening this week, I will prayerfully write in my journal any insights I have about where I see God doing his work of transformation and renovation in my heart and mind. I'll make note of specific instances when I've observed the battle within my heart take place and how the Holy Spirit helped me face and then forsake those idols. I

choose to be encouraged by this newfound sensitivity to sin, because it is proof that God is working to purify my heart for my good and his glory.

3. Self-forgetfulness with God. We are "a people that are his very own, eager to do what is good." As I work to memorize these verses from Titus 2:11–14, I will speak them out loud every morning and evening so that my first and last thoughts of the day focus on the good work God is doing within me. I will write these promises on a card and carry them with me wherever I go, intentionally meditating on these powerful truths until I have internalized them.

Chapter 6

Why God Blesses the Self-Forgetful and Those Who Forgive

Slaves, in reverent fear of God submit yourselves
to your masters, not only to those who are good and
considerate, but also to those who are harsh. For it is
commendable if someone bears up under the pain of
unjust suffering because they are conscious of God. But
how is it to your credit if you receive a beating for doing
wrong and endure it? But if you suffer for doing good
and endure it, this is commendable before God. To this
you were called, because Christ suffered for you, leaving
you an example, that should follow in his steps.

1 Peter 2:18–21

*God has determined that his people would not be marked
by trouble-free lives but by how we trust him during good
times and bad. Trusting him only during overt blessing is
not trusting him at all. The early church knew this well.
When accused falsely or maligned, his people felt honored
because they were found worthy to suffer with and for Jesus.*

Edward Welch

Joseph took charge of the family-run medical supply business his father had founded some three decades earlier. Joseph loved being part of a family-owned endeavor that not only met the financial needs of his immediate family but was successful enough to allow him to generously donate to the needs of others in their small rural community. After his father retired, Joseph's lifelong hope that his son Ben might one day follow in his footsteps became more pronounced. Joseph and Ben had many casual conversations about Ben's possible future after he graduated from college.

Working for the family business in the afternoons and on weekends during the school year and full time during the summer and holidays had been a win-win situation for both Ben and the company. Throughout the final summer after Ben graduated from high school, all was well between him and his dad.

Ben left the weekend before Labor Day for a college two hours south of their home. It didn't take long for him to fall into this new freedom with new friends with more enthusiasm than he showed for his studies. Most days, he slept in late and went to class late, if at all.

Phone calls to and from home grew infrequent, and Joseph's texts to Ben went unanswered for days at a time. Finally, growing ever more concerned about his son, Joseph took a day off and drove down to the college. He had a copy of Ben's class schedule, so he knew where Ben ought to be that particular day. When he arrived at the college, he tried calling Ben, but there was no answer. He texted his son and received no reply. Finally, he went to Ben's dorm room and knocked on the door. Ben answered the door disheveled and hung over from the previous night's indulgences.

What transpired next went down in Joseph's personal history record as one of the most painful conversations he ever had with his son. Once Ben recovered from the immediate shock of seeing his dad standing in his doorway, he became angry. Unlike his usual mellow self, Ben accused his father of not trusting him, not respecting him, not treating him like an adult. Ben then made it clear he'd never consider coming back home to partner with his dad in the business.

Joseph struggled against responding with emotionally charged accusations of his own (truthful though they might have been), wisely waiting until Ben ran out of words. Then he calmly said, "Ben, it's clear that something is going on here. You haven't been going to class. You're failing two courses. And you haven't been answering your phone or responding to any of my texts. I'm worried about you, Son. I want to continue this conversation at a later time. When you come home next weekend for Thanksgiving break, we'll sit down and talk." As he walked back to his car, reflecting on this troubling change in his son, Joseph's heart broke. "Lord, help me," he prayed. "Guide me. Give me the words I need to break through Ben's hardened heart. I can't do this alone."

It's easy to be kind and compassionate to those who are kind and compassionate to us, and respond with cruelty and anger to those who are cruel and angry to us. But Scripture calls us to a much higher standard than that as Christ-followers. Jesus, by his own example, paints a very different picture than returning evil for evil. He always spoke and acted for the eternal benefit, blessing, and instruction of those around him.

As we consider the heartrending conversation between Joseph and his son, it's clear that Ben spewed hateful words at his father out of whatever struggle was going on within his heart. But in his calm, measured response, Joseph reflected Jesus' manner of self-forgetful, forgiveness-driven communication. Joseph emulated the pattern of our Lord, even though he was angrily accused, maligned, and abused. He addressed both the primary issue at hand and the need for further conversation when he and Ben could talk peacefully and respectfully.

Although Joseph's heart was broken after being on the receiving end of Ben's angry onslaught, he wisely sought to meet his son's greater need: he longed to rescue Ben's troubled heart. In humility-driven self-forgetfulness, he knew it was more important to pursue his son's wayward, rebellious heart than to get angry and self-protective in response to Ben's unkindness.

Joseph recognized that even though he was the target of Ben's anger, he didn't have to further escalate the already emotionally volatile situation by volleying back with his own words of aggression. Rather, he chose to speak with purposeful self-forgetfulness accompanied by a forgiving spirit. Did Joseph still desire answers to his valid questions? Yes. But what he wanted most of all was an opportunity to dialogue with his son about matters of the heart. When Joseph patiently waited for the proper time, God blessed his efforts. The following weekend after that painful scene, Joseph and Ben had a long talk about what was really going on in Ben's heart and mind. Both father and son spoke. They both listened. Then Ben asked for Joseph's forgiveness, and father and son were reconciled.

Take-away Action Thought

When I am on the receiving end of someone's anger, I will ask God to help me see the bigger picture. I will ask him to help me respond in a way that demonstrates that my primary concern is the person's eternal welfare. God will give me the grace to not retaliate in anger but to respond with compassion, kindness, and gentleness.

My Heart's Cry to You, O Lord

Father, I can still hear the hate-filled words in my mind. It hurts so much to be treated this way. I'm trying to understand if there was anything I did to provoke such a personal attack. Please help me to set aside my wounded emotions and give me the grace to pray for my attacker's best. Show me the path to reconciliation. Whatever happens, Lord, I need your eternal perspective for this troubling situation. I rely on your grace and strength to offer self-forgetful love and genuine forgiveness. Amen.

Finding Joyful Freedom in Self-forgetfulness

1. Self-forgetfulness with others. "In reverent fear of God submit yourselves." I will prayerfully ask God to bring to my mind any instances where I have held onto resentment. If I have done so, then I will confess this sin.

2. Self-forgetfulness in me. "It is commendable if some-
    one bears up under the pain of unjust suffering." Be-
    cause of Jesus' perfect sacrifice on the cross for my sins,
    I will intentionally try to be self-forgetful rather than
    self-protective. I'll ask God to help me respond more
    like Jesus in the coming days by placing my well-being
    into his care and striving to forgive others obediently
    and swiftly.

3. Self-forgetfulness with God. "Christ suffered for you,
    leaving you an example." Each evening this week, I will
    reflect on the day and ask God to reveal to me if I used
    every opportunity to bring others closer to his saving
    love. I will pray nightly for the grace to set aside my
    own wants and desires and place others' needs above
    my own.

Chapter 7

God Empowers Those Who Live to Serve

God is our refuge and strength, an ever-present help
in trouble. Therefore we will not fear, though the
earth give way and the mountains fall into the heart
of the sea, though its waters roar and foam and the
mountains quake with their surging. . . . The LORD
Almighty is with us; the God of Jacob is our fortress.

Psalm 46:1–3, 7

*God alone is our refuge. He gives two kinds of help. He is a
stronghold into which we can flee, and He is a source of inner
strength by which we can face every trial. God is my personal
refuge, your personal refuge. Our God is all-sufficient; His
defense can surpass that of any and every enemy. And
what does our personal refuge promise us? There is no time,
situation, or trial for which He does not send His help.*

Linda Dillow

A mong her friends, Carrie was known as a master gardener who always had handy a fresh bouquet of flowers
or greenery to give away. Her floral gifts were treasured

by their happy recipients because they were daily reminders of love, life, and beauty that kept on giving day after day. Her stunning home garden inspired everyone who glimpsed its luscious and bountiful beauty.

In reality, of course, Carrie's garden took a lot of hard work to keep it flourishing. Despite all the labor she invested in her flowers, the real joy came from the time she was able to talk with God in her beautiful garden. It was on her knees pulling weeds that she prayed for her family, friends, and neighbors. It was while she was watering her plants that she sang joyfully to the Lord. It was in her garden that she sensed God's refuge, strength, and ever-present help. God had indeed blessed Carrie with a gift for growing beautiful flowers. But more importantly, she had learned to labor hard with that gift so that she could bless others in need of special encouragement. And God did indeed bless Carrie's efforts and her self-sacrifice.

What made Carrie's special service to others even more remarkable was that, unknown to most of her friends, she was in her second battle against breast cancer. She was worn out and tired from the cancer treatments she received each week at the medical center. Her oncologist warned against pushing herself too hard, but she told him that she felt most alive and closest to the Lord while in the garden doing what she loved.

She heeded his advice to take a long nap every afternoon and to shorten her labor in the garden. But she soon realized that her spiritual well-being seemed to correspond with how much time she was able to spend there, nurturing and caring for it. Certainly, she had difficult days when she was exhausted, anxious, and fearful about her cancer. But she also recognized the healing power that comes from enjoying God's beautiful creation and self-forgetfully taking part in sharing its wonders with others. For Carrie, her garden was the place where she found God's presence and his help. In turn, God gave her the strength to give that same gift to others.

Psalm 46 is one of my favorite portions of Scripture because the psalmist's wording is so wonderfully comforting in its description of who God is and who he promises to be for us when we face trials of any kind. God is our refuge and strength, an ever-present help in trouble. As Linda Dillow puts it, "There is no time, situation, or trial for which He does not send His help." Amazing!

As we lean into the promises of Psalm 46 and meditate on their comforting truths, we find ourselves exhaling whatever fears, worries, and anxieties are plaguing our thoughts today. Close your eyes and mentally drink in the picture of who God is to us as his beloved children. God is our refuge. God is our strength. God is our ever-present help in time of trouble.

Then take this powerful promise a step further, as Carrie did. Though she was facing cancer for a second time, she intentionally sought out the place and posture to find her renewed strength and peace in God. While not all of us can have a garden retreat as Carrie did, we can all find somewhere to be still before the Lord and allow his Holy Spirit to bring to our remembrance his present promises and reminders of his past faithfulness.

As we quiet our emotions and rest, we find the strength that God provides to reach out in self-forgetful acts of love and service to others. We can do this! Even when we're unsure about the outcomes of our own trials, God gives us the strength to turn our love outward in blessing others.

Take-away Action Thought

When I feel afraid and anxious about a present trial in my life, I will find a quiet place to retreat to so I can allow God's comforting promises to be my refuge, my strength, and an ever-present help. I will take all the time I need to allow this powerful truth to sink deeply into my heart and mind.

My Heart's Cry to You, O Lord

Father, I come to you in need of your comfort and strength. I'm going through a trial I hoped I would never face again. But in your sovereignty, you have allowed this season of suffering to reenter my life. Please help me to lay all my fears, worries, and anxieties at your feet. Give me the grace to leave them there. And then, please help me get back on my feet and notice those in need of love and encouragement. By faith, I will use all the gifts, talents, and resources you have given me to bring blessings to others today. Amen.

Finding Joyful Freedom in Self-forgetfulness

1. Self-forgetfulness with others. "God is our refuge and strength, an ever-present help in trouble." Even though I'm facing my own severe trials, I will prayerfully ask the Lord to bring to mind someone who needs a word of encouragement this week. I will spend time praying for this person and make contact by writing a note, emailing, texting, or calling to tell them I'm standing with them in prayer.

2. Self-forgetfulness in me. "Therefore, we will not fear." My greatest temptation is to become so caught up in fear and worry over my own trials that I forget that everyone is struggling with something. I will pray for God to give me the sensitivity and grace to live this week in a truly self-forgetful way, even though I'm not sure of my own outcome. I will seek the Lord so that I'm ready to reach out toward others in their distress with the good news of the gospel.

3. Self-forgetfulness with God. "The LORD Almighty is with us." As part of my daily Bible reading, I will do a word search on "Almighty" and study the verses that use this descriptive expression of God. I'll write down the verses that stand out to me and commit two to memory.

Chapter 8

Self-Forgetfulness – In the Home

As a prisoner for the Lord, then, I urge you to live
a life worthy of the calling you have received. Be
completely humble and gentle; be patient, bearing
with one another in love. Make every effort to keep
the unity of the Spirit through the bond of peace.

Ephesians 4:1–3

*Humility always seeks, like Jesus, to be the servant, the
helper, and the comforter of others, even to the lowest and
most unworthy. Let us look upon everyone who tries us as
God's means of grace, God's instrument for our purification,
for our exercise of the humility of Jesus. May we have true
faith in the sufficiency of God and admit to the inefficiency
of self, that by God's power we will serve one another in love.*

Andrew Murray

By the time the police arrived at their home, Ellen and
Jon were beside themselves about their missing teenage son Jon Jr., who didn't come home last night. He
had told them he had the late shift at the fast-food restaurant
where he worked, so they went to bed unconcerned. Since it

was a Saturday, Ellen let her son sleep in later than the usual weekday schedule.

She then got busy with her Saturday morning house cleaning and laundry chores while Jon went outside to do some yard work. After finishing up, Ellen realized she hadn't yet seen or heard from Jon Jr. that morning. When she knocked on his bedroom door, he didn't answer. Quietly opening the door in case he was still asleep, she saw that his bed hadn't been slept in. Then she noticed that some of his clothes were missing, along with his laptop and other personal items. Ellen's heart plummeted. *Not again*, she despaired.

She hurried outside to tell her husband: "He's gone! He ran away again!" Ellen trembled as her voice broke. Jon marched into the house to call the police. While Ellen could only weep, Jon was visibly angry and frustrated.

Upset by his escalating reaction, she pleaded with him: "We have to settle down, Jon. We have to hold it together so we can explain to the police what happened. Please calm down." Turning around, he yelled at her, "Do *not* tell me how to respond to our son's reckless behavior! This is the last time he's going to put us through this foolishness! And don't think I don't notice how you always take his side whenever I try to discipline him! His attention-getting games are over!"

Just when Ellen didn't think she could feel any worse, the police car drove up. Taking a deep breath and uttering a silent prayer for strength and grace, she greeted the officers and invited them inside. Together, she hoped, they could locate Jon Jr., get him home, and begin the repair work of untangling the mess that was their family.

Although blame-shifting has been happening since the Garden of Eden, it never solves the heart issues of whatever conflict we're mired in. It's easy to fall into this ungodly, unloving response when suddenly faced with the unthinkable. No one can fully understand the immediate panic-stricken, heart-plummeting response a parent experiences when one of their children goes missing. Since I've been in a similar situation, I can see how easy it was for Jon to become angry with his son and yet take out all that anger on his wife, simply because she was present and Jon Jr. wasn't.

Years ago, when our daughter went missing overnight and we called in our local police to help us find her, Jim and I experienced the same gamut of emotional responses as Ellen and Jon. Both of us vacillated between despair and hope, anger and love, frustration and acceptance, worry and peace. It would have been so easy for us to blame the other for her poor choices. But pointing the finger at someone never accomplishes anything, does it? Even if our failure might in part be true, we need to give and receive loving support if we are to survive a crisis.

In our homes, we should be working toward a consistent attitude of self-forgetfulness that begins with our inner posture toward one another, even in difficult circumstances. We embrace an attitude of self-forgetful humility when we learn to see those who irritate and injure us as "instruments of God's purification." Only when we know we belong to Jesus and trust that our best interests are always in the forefront of his care for us can we humbly, gently, and compassionately turn the other cheek when wrongly accused. Let's be clear: Jesus is not advocating abuse of any kind. Rather, our Savior and Lord asks us to bear with one another in love and pursue peace as much as we are able.

Ellen realized from long experience how Jon tended to express his anger in a way that hurt her, but she also knew he would calm down and ask her forgiveness. And she would give it. Ellen also knew (from long experience) how many times she had allowed her own emotions to spiral out of control only to hurt those she loved with harsh and unkind words. Ellen and Jon made peace with each other, and then they worked on creating a plan to make those same peaceful reparations with their wayward son. "Bearing with one another in love" had always been their parental position with their son—and it always would be.

Take-away Action Thought

When I feel my emotions begin to spiral out of control, I will remove myself from the volatile situation and go to a quiet place where I can seek the Lord's guidance. I will not reenter the emotionally charged scenario until I have calmed and composed myself.

My Heart's Cry to You, O Lord

Father, here I am in the same awful situation I've been in before. I feel like I'm in an emotional free fall. There seems to be no end in sight. And the worst part of this heartache is that I'm tempted to blame my spouse for something our child has done. I know this is wrong. Please help me to calm down and put all my trust in you and you alone. Help me to step back from this situation and hand it over to you. I want to be humble, gentle, patient, and long-suffering, but I have so much to learn. Dear Lord, show me the way to peace within and with others. Amen.

Finding Joyful Freedom in Self-forgetfulness

1. Self-forgetfulness with others. "Be completely humble and gentle; be patient, bearing with one another in love." This week, I will take daily emotion temperature checks at the end of the day, making note of how I treated those in my family. I will determine to be more self-forgetful in my emotional responses toward my family, friends, and others.

2. Self-forgetfulness in me. "Live a life worthy of the calling you have received." Each day this week, I will spend some quiet moments contemplating what it means to be "a prisoner of the Lord." I will look up in my Bible all the verses that contain the word *prisoner* for further study so I can better grasp what this word really means to me on a day-by-day basis.

3. Self-forgetfulness with God. "Make every effort to keep the unity of the Spirit through the bond of peace." During my quiet times with the Lord, I will ask myself these questions:

   - Am I living peaceably with those in my family?
   - Am I doing my best to live peaceably with my friends?
   - Am I seeking peace with those I don't agree with?

   If I'm faltering in these areas, I'll ask a wise friend to help keep me accountable as I seek to live a more self-forgetful, peaceable life with others.

Chapter 9

Self-Forgetfulness – In the Workplace

I have chosen the way of faithfulness; I have set my
heart on your laws. I hold fast to your statutes, LORD;
do not let me be put to shame. I run in the path of your
commands, for you have broadened my understanding.

Psalm 119:30–32

*Our first priority in times of adversity is to honor and glorify
God by trusting Him. We tend to make our first priority
the gaining of relief from our feelings of heartache or
disappointment or frustration. This is a natural desire, and
God has promised to give us grace sufficient for our trials
and peace for our anxieties. We honor God by choosing to
trust Him when we don't understand what He is doing or
why He has allowed some adverse circumstance to occur.*

Jerry Bridges

Nora was in the final countdown of her long and beloved
career at the post office. She'd never intended to retire
before the age of sixty-five; then again, she'd never expected to assume the full-time care of her recently disabled
sister. But when she received that ominous phone call some

eight months ago, everything changed: Camille, her elder sister, had been in an automobile accident that had left her almost completely paralyzed from the waist down. Nora faithfully made sure Camille received the best care while in the hospital and during her stay in the rehabilitation center. But when at long last Camille was able to go home, it was obvious she would still need a great deal of assistance.

It fell on Nora to make the decision of where Camille would live after being released from the rehabilitation home. Nora's single-story, four-bedroom home made a whole lot more sense than Camille's two-story farmhouse, which provided limited space to maneuver her bulky wheelchair. After giving it much thought and prayer, Nora invited Camille to share her home with her, an offer Camille gratefully accepted. Nora initially felt immense relief after making that momentous decision. Soon, however, she started to struggle with persistent negative thoughts that dampened her spirits and her day-to-day attitude.

I know this is the best possible solution for Camille, she thought. *But why am I finding it so hard to accept my early retirement? I realize it will be a lot cheaper for me to help with her daytime care rather than hiring 24/7 nursing help. And I did have only another twelve months before I planned to retire. But those twelve months meant something to me.*

She realized something else: *I've become a cranky old woman since I put in my official retirement notice. I know this is true because everyone is giving me wide berth at the office. If I don't make an about-face attitude change, my colleagues will be glad to see the back of me.*

"Oh Lord," Nora prayed, "help me to make peace with my decision. Give me the grace to stop taking out my personal disappointment on those I still have time to love and influence for you. This might not have been my plan—but it's clearly yours. Please broaden my understanding of your will so I can get in step with it."

"Broaden my understanding." What fitting words to cling to and pray for whenever we face circumstances beyond our comprehension! Each of us will have to deal with unexpected life-altering events that leave us struggling to make sense of. Like Nora, we will all be given the opportunity to choose the path of self-forgetfulness. Despite the right choice of inviting her sister into her spacious home and taking an earlier retirement than she planned, she felt the sting of sadness and disappointment. Who wouldn't?

And yet, Nora quickly identified her disappointment with her current crankiness and realized she still had precious time left that she could use to invest in her colleagues of many years. She wisely knew she needed to end her career at the post office well. She wanted to spend her remaining work hours serving, encouraging, and blessing everyone she came into contact with while she still could. Nora understood that self-forgetfulness isn't limited to the home front. While her coworkers praised her for her selflessness with regard to Camille, her selfless sacrifices wouldn't pack much of a powerful punch if she took out her disappointment on those she worked with every day.

Ending well, therefore, became Nora's goal. She wanted to leave her productive career with a clean conscience and no regrets. Most of all, she wanted her colleagues to remember her as a woman who trusted in her faithful God no matter what challenges, struggles, and trials came her way. Like the psalmist, Nora wholeheartedly chose "the way of faithfulness," and God blessed her for it.

Take-away Action Thought

When I feel the sting of disappointment, I will recount all the ways God has met me in my time of need. I will be a good remember-er even in this difficult moment when I don't understand what is happening. I will talk to God about how I am feeling and then commit myself anew to his perfect care and keeping—for today and for all my tomorrows.

My Heart's Cry to You, O Lord

Father, this morning I woke up with a headache from over-thinking my recent decisions. I keep replaying in my mind what I had originally planned and how different my life is becoming from what I had hoped. Honestly, I am feeling sad and disappointed. I know I made the best choices for going forward, but my heart aches for what might have been. Please help me to cling to your precious promises in the days that follow. Help me to follow the path of intentional self-forgetfulness so I can continue to love, serve, and encourage all those you bring my way. I want to embrace this new season full of your grace and strength, even if it's not what I had planned. My confidence is in you and your perfect provision for me. Amen.

Finding Joyful Freedom in Self-Forgetfulness

1. Self-forgetfulness with others. "I have chosen the way of faithfulness." Each day this week, I will choose a different coworker to bless and encourage. I'll make sure to plan ahead so I have the time and opportunity to truly

find a creative way to love each of these individuals. These small acts of blessing might include taking over a task, offering a word of encouragement, or bringing in a favorite snack or beverage.

2. Self-forgetfulness in me. "I have set my heart on your laws." Each evening this week, I will read a chapter from the book of Proverbs that corresponds with the day on the calendar. I will slowly and prayerfully read through each daily proverb, mindful of how often the principle of self-forgetfulness appears in this book about wise living.

3. Self-forgetfulness with God. "You have broadened my understanding." Using my journal, I will write down at least one account (past or present) of God's specific faithfulness toward me during a time when I didn't understand what was going to happen or how my trial might unfold. At the end of the week, I will reread these journal entries and spend time thanking God for his perfect provision for me.

Chapter 10

Self-Forgetfulness – In Our Churches

Consider it pure joy, my brothers and sisters, whenever
you face trials of many kinds, because you know that
the testing of your faith produces perseverance. Let
perseverance finish its work so that you may be mature
and complete, not lacking anything. If any of you lacks
wisdom, you should ask God, who gives generously to
all without finding fault, and it will be given to you.

James 1:2–5

*Perhaps in hard moments, when we are tempted to wonder
where God's grace is, it is grace that we are getting, but
not grace in the form of a soft pillow or a cool drink.
Rather, in those moments, we are being blessed with the
heart-transforming grace of difficulty because the God who
loves us knows that this is exactly the grace we need.*

Paul David Tripp

Stacy eyed the pews to her left in search of the three senior citizen friends with whom she shared a lunch every
Sunday after church. There they sat, her three elderly,

delightful, fun-loving gal pals. Looking across the large sanctuary, she smiled fondly at her friends, taking note of how they whispered to one another and then laughed quietly or nudged each other gently and pointed when something new or different caught their eye. Based on appearances alone, no one would guess that Stacy had anything in common with Ruth, Mary, and Maude, who were all older than her own mom would have been if she were still alive.

What most people didn't know was that the four women had bonded over shared tragedy. Stacy, now a young widow at fifty-four, had discovered kindred spirits in these three elderly widows soon after her husband Scott had passed away. She recalled with affection how each of these loving women had sent her their personal condolences through letters and cards over a six-month period. With every note Stacy received, she realized that Ruth, Mary, and Maude all understood her pain in ways most others didn't. After a time, Stacy took the initiative and started taking them out to lunch every Sunday.

For the better part of two years, these four friends in faith and widowhood had shared many a good laugh, a smattering of tears, and lots of hard-won wisdom over lingering cups of coffee and tea. This weekly ritual was so personally enriching that it often became the highlight of Stacy's week. That is, until both Ruth and Mary started showing increasing signs of Alzheimer's disease. As time passed, Stacy and Maude began to exchange knowing looks whenever either of these women said or did something out of character. It was heartbreaking to witness the escalating decline of their friends. Eventually, Stacy had to acknowledge that Ruth and Mary were no longer the winsome and mentally sharp women she had come to know and love.

After one particularly troubling luncheon conversation, Stacy and Maude met together and shared their mutual feelings of sadness and loss at the mental decline of their friends.

Stacy admitted how difficult it was to observe Ruth's and Mary's increasingly confused states up close and personal. "This loss feels too much like what I felt when I lost Scott," she confessed. "And I'm not sure I can go through that pain again."

Stacy then shared how thankful she had been when God brought these three widows into her life at a time when she needed their godly influence and encouragement the most. But now, it just plain hurt to see them unable to think or communicate the way they used to do. Maude listened quietly to her before replying: "Stacy, dear, I feel the same sadness and loss you're experiencing. But we need to remember that God already knew the changes that were going to happen in both Ruth and Mary. Have you considered that God brought us all together to take turns lifting each other up? I know it's hard to watch loved ones decline, but isn't this the perfect time to keep reminding them how much we care?"

Loss upon loss. That single refrain ran through Stacy's mind after she left Maude that day. She wondered why God would allow her to grow so close to these three faithful women only to have to grieve the loss of two of them. Stacy talked to God about the heartache she felt over losing her dear friends so soon after losing her husband. It just felt like too much loss for one person to handle. It would be much easier, she felt, if she distanced herself from the mental decline of her friends. But that would certainly not be in the best interests of either Stacy or her three friends. And God was already revealing that truth to Stacy's hurting heart.

Have you ever faced a situation like Stacy's? Maybe you experienced all the blessings and the benefits of service in your church community, only for that happy dynamic to suddenly change. Did you feel like giving up? Did you believe you didn't have what it took to keep on serving, giving, and loving? Stacy initially reacted self-protectively when she admitted how much simpler it would be to put some distance between herself and her ailing friends. But in her heart of hearts, she also knew that the path God had placed her on was one that required consistent self-forgetfulness.

We can trust that God in his all-knowing wisdom will do what is best for us in order to conform us into the image of his son, Jesus. Often, the grace God gives us doesn't come in the form of "a soft pillow or a cool drink." Rather, he gives grace that perseveres and is strong, mature, complete, and dependable.

When we find ourselves facing painful challenges, we want to run in the opposite direction and respond instead by falling on our knees in humble prayer. May we stay there until God restores, replenishes, and revitalizes our hearts and minds to stay with the self-forgetful task he has appointed us to complete.

Take-away Action Thought

When I start to feel my emotions succumbing to paralyzing sorrow, pain, and loss and I feel like quitting, I will return to this passage in James 1 and meditate on it. I will spend all the time I need before the Lord in prayer, asking for his grace and strength and a fresh new perspective to stay the course he has placed me on.

My Heart's Cry to You, O Lord

Father, today I found myself tempted to give up and quit this ministry you have given me. In the past, I felt confident that you directed me to serve my church in this way. But now it feels like everything is changing too quickly for my emotions to keep up. I admit that in the beginning, I was the one who was blessed and encouraged. But now, I see that you may be calling me to bear a heavy burden for these dear folks. Help me to stay on the path you have appointed for me, even if I do experience pangs of sorrow and loss. I rely solely on your grace, your strength, and your divine wisdom to equip me to love and serve in your stead. Amen.

Finding Joyful Freedom in Self-Forgetfulness

1. Self-forgetfulness with others. "Consider it pure joy, my brothers and sisters, whenever you face trials of many kinds." Each day this week, I will prayerfully consider the most pressing needs of those with whom I have been ministering. I will then find a way to practically meet one need at a time as God enables me.

2. Self-forgetfulness in me. "Let perseverance finish its work so that you may be mature and complete, not lacking anything." This week, I will spend time journaling about my service and ministry to my church family. I'll write down the many blessings and benefits (as well as the challenges and hardships) of serving that God has revealed to me and how I have been refined in the process.

3. Self-forgetfulness with God. "If any of you lacks wisdom, you should ask God." Each morning this week, I will begin my prayer time by asking God to give me the wisdom I need for that day's work and service to others.

Chapter 11

Self-Forgetfulness – In Our Neighborhoods

What good is it, my brothers and sisters, if someone
claims to have faith but has no deeds? Can such faith save
them? Suppose a brother or a sister is without clothes
and daily food. If one of you says to them, "Go in peace;
keep warm and well fed," but does nothing about their
physical needs, what good is it? In the same way, faith
by itself, if it is not accompanied by action, is dead.

James 2:14–17

*Mercy has eyes. It pays attention to your distress and
notices your weaknesses and failures. But mercy looks at
these things with eyes of compassion. It doesn't criticize
you for the tough situation you are in or condemn you
for your sin. Mercy wants to relieve your suffering and
forgive your debt. It looks for ways to help you out of your
struggle and remove your guilt and shame. Real mercy
is restless. It is not content with the status quo. It doesn't
rest until things are better for you. It works hard, costs
a lot, and is ready to hang on until the job is done.*

Tim Lane and Paul David Tripp

K arley felt a twinge of shame as she ducked out her front door to grab her mail and then right back in again, hoping that her neighbor Crissy hadn't spotted her. It had been a hectic, demanding week, and Karley had more tasks waiting for her attention than she had time or energy to complete. Shutting the door and locking it, she felt the familiar ache of discomfort she had come to associate with her neighbor and sadly thought to herself, *I've become a prisoner in my home.*

Crissy had four elementary-aged children over whom she hovered in a fear-driven, obsessive manner. Crissy was so terrified for their physical health and safety, as well as their mental and emotional well-being, that she was unknowingly creating fearful and worried mini-versions of herself in each of her children. Karley had spent many afternoons trying to counsel Crissy and encourage her to work through her ungoverned fears. She prayed for and with Crissy. Together, they opened the Bible, and she shared with Crissy numerous verses that highlighted the peace God desires for his children. But it seemed to no avail.

After a few months of unending phone calls and texts day and night and unexpected visits at the most inopportune times, Crissy had worn Karley down. Although Karley had tried to help Crissy work through her continual liturgy of scary and often outlandish "what ifs," Crissy never once followed through on any of Karley's suggestions for dealing with her out-of-control fears. Karley was now at her wits' end. How could she continue to serve and minister to her neighbor if Crissy was as unreasonable with her expectations of Karley as she was about her children's welfare?

Karley sat down, opened her Bible to the book of James, and began reading. She prayed for God's wisdom and understanding. "Lord, I want to be of help to my neighbor, but what I'm doing right now isn't making any difference at all. She isn't responding to your word's challenges about changing her thoughts or her actions. She's stuck and so am I! I want to reach out with your truth and your love, but I need to change my tactics. Give me fresh insight on how to help this woman without losing my mind and my peace in the process. Amen."

If only we could serve our neighbors in five easy steps and then proceed to neatly tie up their problems in a box and toss it into the trash. It may be nice to daydream about such streamlined acts of service, but we all know that's not how life works! Karley's heart attitude toward her neighbor was a humble, God-honoring one. She longed to see Crissy set free from her worries, fears, and compulsions. She was doing her best to be self-forgetful toward Crissy despite the fact that Crissy regularly crossed reasonable boundaries, leaving Karley with nothing to show for her investment in Crissy's life.

Overwhelmed as she was, Karley didn't want to give up on her neighbor. Though she was worn out from Crissy's incessant neediness, she was being driven to a deciding point on how to effectively help her. Thankfully, Karley took her cares and burdens to the Lord and to his word, where she found good counsel for herself. She was determined to continue acting on her words of faith on behalf of her neighbor, but the scenario for serving would look different going forward.

After resting her weary mind and emotions, Karley was able to see the problem in a fresh light. She thanked the Lord for helping her devise a more effective and workable plan. In the coming days, Karley set a regular time each week to meet with Crissy for Bible study and prayer, and she explained to Crissy that accountability was key to real heart and life change. Together, they began memorizing verses of Scripture. Then,

Karley reminded Crissy that she had her own husband, children, home, and church responsibilities. Karley made it clear that she would no longer answer the phone during mealtimes or weekends—and that Crissy's texts might go unanswered if she sent them too frequently. Firm boundaries, Karley realized, was the only way she could continue to effectively serve Crissy over the long haul.

It took some time, of course, for Crissy to accept that Karley meant what she said. But Karley knew that if she continued to make herself available day in and day out, then Crissy would never learn to go directly to the Lord for help. By taking specific but small steps out of Crissy's life, Karley recognized that Crissy would have no alternative but to seek God's wisdom for herself. It was a win-win for them both. Over time, Karley was able to witness real evidence of spiritual growth in her neighbor, which began to change Crissy's thinking, her attitudes, and her family dynamics—all for her good and God's glory.

 Take-away Action Thought

When I begin to feel overwhelmed by the challenges of serving, I will retreat to a quiet place, open God's word, and pray about the situation. I will ask the Lord to give me fresh insight and ideas about serving in a self-forgetful way so that I don't suffer from burnout.

My Heart's Cry to You, O Lord

Father, I'm finding myself irritable and impatient with everyone because I'm so overwhelmed by my neighbor's neediness. I feel stuck in a never-ending cycle of frustration on behalf of both of us. I want to scream, "I never signed up for this!" The truth is, I want to love and serve my neighbor, but I have to learn to do so in a way that doesn't take over my entire life. Please give me fresh insight on effective ways to tackle this problem. I ask for your wisdom, because I am out of my depth. Amen.

Finding Joyful Freedom in Self-Forgetfulness

1. Self-forgetfulness with others. "What good is it, my brothers and sisters, if someone claims to have faith but has no deeds?" I will make note of my neighbor's most pressing needs, whether they are physical, emotional, or spiritual. Next, I will create a practical plan to meet two of these needs in the coming week.

2. Self-forgetfulness in me. "If one of you says to them, 'Go in peace; keep warm and well fed,' but does nothing about their physical needs, what good is it?" During prayer, I'll ask the Lord to reveal my heart motives about serving my neighbor. If I'm serving with a poor attitude, I will confess this sin, ask for forgiveness, and pray for grace to begin again with a self-forgetful mindset.

3. Self-forgetfulness with God. "Faith by itself, if it is not accompanied by action, is dead." This week, I will note in my journal about the previous experiences I've had when I was positioned to serve one-on-one. I'll make a special effort to recall both my heart attitude in those situations and what I did practically to love each individual. I want to make the connection between a rightful heart attitude and the self-forgetful actions that follow.

 *Chapter 12*

Self-Forgetfulness – With Our Families

We who are strong ought to bear with the failings of the weak
and not to please ourselves. . . . May the God who gives
endurance and encouragement give you the same attitude
of mind toward each other that Christ Jesus had, so that
with one mind and one voice you may glorify the God and
Father of our Lord Jesus Christ. Accept one another, then,
just as Christ accepted you, in order to bring praise to God.

Romans 15:1, 5–7

*Anger takes everything personally, as if everything is
an intentional act to make your life miserable. You
react in anger because you would not have made that
mistake. But wise people, patient people, are willing to
say "wait" to their anger, and then study the other person.
They ask these kind of questions: "What happened? Why
didn't you do what you said you would do?" "Help me
to understand what you were thinking when you did
that." "How can I help you the next time this happens?"*

Edward Welch

Finding his son looking in the refrigerator for something to eat, Kirk asked him the question of the day: "Kyle, why didn't you clean up the basement before you left to go play ball with your friends? Explain it to me."

Kyle continued to stare into the fridge rather than look his dad in the eye—not after he had messed up again. He really had intended to get up early Saturday morning and clean the basement before he did anything else. But he had forgotten. He'd gotten a call from his best friend Tim in the middle of breakfast, asking him to come right over. Apparently, the neighborhood teens had decided to host a last-minute baseball tournament at the field behind their school. Insistent, Tim begged Kyle to hurry up, grab his mitt and bat, and join them.

Kyle couldn't explain exactly what happened between his last bite of cereal and Tim's phone call and then his sprint to the garage to get his gear. Some four hours later, Kyle happily returned through the garage door and hung up his bat, tossed his mitt on the upper shelf, and went straight to the fridge for a snack. After all, running bases and catching fly balls makes a kid hungry! Staring into the depths of the refrigerator while his mind replayed the last few runs that had won his team the final game, Kyle didn't hear his dad enter the kitchen.

Kirk cleared his throat and repeated the question: "*Kyle, did you hear me?*" Kyle finally turned around and sheepishly said, "Sorry, Dad. I really did plan on cleaning it first thing, like you told me. Then Tim called and I forgot. I'll go downstairs right now and do it."

Kirk didn't say a word. He simply stood there. But inside his mind was a mix of frustration, irritation, and confusion. In truth, he and Kyle were so different in personality that he struggled to understand his son. Kirk was structured, organized, and self-disciplined, and couldn't imagine leaving a chore unfinished if his parents had issued an order. However, he had been down this path with Kyle before and knew better than to respond with overt anger or harsh words. Instead, Kirk gave his son a greater gift: the gift of grace. "Okay, Son. Just get down there now and finish up before dinner."

Kyle breathed a grateful sigh of relief and nodded his thanks as he passed his dad on the stairs down to the basement.

This is a fine example of what self-forgetfulness looks like in the day-to-day interchanges of family life. I am both humbled and encouraged by Kirk's loving-kindness toward his son. Self-forgetfulness "family-style" involves overlooking the little things to keep the main things in their proper place. Kirk was keenly aware that his son was different from himself in many ways. He realized that he wasn't "better" or "more worthy" than his son simply because he wasn't similar to him in personality and giftedness. Kirk also wisely understood that as Kyle's father, he had a responsibility to parent Kyle to independent, mature adulthood, which meant there needed to be consequences for poor choices.

The difficulty within the family dynamic, especially between parents and children (and sometimes between husbands and wives), is that we frequently do misunderstand each other because we think differently. We may view the same circumstance through our own unique lenses, and we might prioritize our tasks differently, to the total bafflement of our loved ones. This is why intentional self-forgetfulness in the home can make all the difference between living on a battlefield and living in a loving, safe, and nurturing environment.

The brief passage from Romans at the beginning of this chapter admonishes us as fellow believers to "accept one another, then, just as Christ accepted you." We must learn this mindset of intentional self-forgetfulness before we enter into the fray of minor conflicts with the people we live with, lest we react sinfully and create an even larger distance between ourselves and our family. To paraphrase Edward Welch, anger takes everything personally, but wisdom knows better. The wise and self-forgetful person understands that God has wired us each differently and that we must learn to study others to better understand the motives behind their attitudes and actions. When we step back and don't react in anger, but instead wisely consider and pray, we are much more likely to bridge the gaps that might otherwise cause misunderstanding and relational disaster.

 ## *Take-away Action Thought*

When I am tempted to become angry and express my frustrations to my family, I will stop myself. I will not speak to others until I have first spoken to God. I will ask God to give me wisdom and understanding so that I can better love and serve those within my home.

My Heart's Cry to You, O Lord

Father, it happened again. I feel as though the same scenario happens over and over again, and I'm tired of traveling on the merry-go-round of this same issue. I feel as though my family member is not paying close enough attention when I speak. Please give me the wisdom and understanding I need to love those within my home unconditionally. Help me to accept each person's unique differences. Clothe me with humility, Lord.

Create in me a spirit of thankfulness, because it is a privilege to have a family to love and invest in. Amen.

Finding Joyful Freedom in Self-Forgetfulness

1. Self-forgetfulness with others. "We who are strong ought to bear with the failings of the weak and not to please ourselves." This week, I will write down the names of each person who lives in my home (or the names of those I spend the most time with outside of my home). I'll list their strengths and weaknesses and begin praying and praising God for their unique personality traits and character qualities. I will focus on giving thanks for the strengths I see in them, and I will verbally commend each one when I see them using these for the good of others.

2. Self-forgetfulness in me. "May the God who gives endurance and encouragement give you the same attitude of mind toward each other that Christ Jesus had." I will make a list of my own strengths and weaknesses. Then I will spend time each evening praying for the Lord to continue to work within my life as I seek to become conformed day by day to the image of Jesus.

3. Self-forgetfulness with God. "Accept one another, then, just as Christ accepted you, in order to bring praise to God." Each morning this week, as part of my quiet time, I will look up a Scripture verse that proclaims God's great gift of salvation. I will meditate on this amazing and eternal gift of life through Jesus to help me have proper perspective about living a self-forgetful life with my family.

Chapter 13

Self-Forgetfulness – With Our Friends

For our struggle is not against flesh and blood, but against
rulers, against the authorities, against the powers of this
dark world and against the spiritual forces of evil in the
heavenly realms. Therefore put on the full armor of God, so
that when the day of evil comes, you may be able to stand
your ground, and after you have done everything, to stand.

Ephesians 6:12–13

*Life is war. A dramatic conflict is underway between the
forces of the Great Speaker and the Great Deceiver. While
God is seeking to root us deeper in his life, his peace, and
his truth, Satan seeks to uproot us by deceitful scheming,
plausible lies, and cruel trickery. Like all wars, this war is
for control. It is a war for our hearts. And if this spiritual
war were not going on, there would be no war of words.*

Paul David Tripp

Ashley and Megan were placed in charge of the new food
pantry being launched by their city-central church. Both
women believed this was a much-needed ministry to
benefit the people who lived on the surrounding streets of their

church building. From the outset, Ashley and Megan had mutually agreed on the planning and the set-up, as well as the day-to-day organization and running the ministry.

After their church's governing board gave them the go-ahead to launch the food pantry, Ashley and Megan began planning for the next several months. Ashley, a former accountant, naturally took to establishing the monthly financial details as a matter of ease. Megan, a PR professional turned stay-at-home mom, headed up the volunteer hiring and training while supervising the actual running of the ministry two mornings a week.

At first, the new ministry ran smoothly—although numerous fellow believers had warned them to expect pushback from the spiritual forces that always oppose Christ's church and his good news. Both women recalled those wise warnings and made a commitment to pray consistently for protection, wisdom, insight, and divine grace every week. They thanked God for the obvious blessing of being able to meet both practical and spiritual needs in their church's surrounding community. When opposition did arrive, it wasn't in the form of a direct and open attack. Instead, it was far more insidious and almost closed down the food pantry ministry before it could be resolved.

Here's what happened: Ashley, the numbers guru, discovered that some of their regular clients were double and triple dipping into the food pantry's free resources by sending in more than one family member to receive food and household goods. When Ashley learned of this rule violation, she quickly developed a more stringent process for needy families to receive their food. The way she saw it, more families would be served if each family received their single portion of resources. This was all well and good until Megan, the self-declared softy of the two friends, viewed the situation differently.

Megan begged Ashley to change the strict new rules. She saw the situation from a more personal point of view. "How can we ever prove that a family is really bending the rules? Maybe they need the extra food for their extended family that lives with them. Have we considered that?" But Ashley was insistent. "The food pantry won't be able to sustain these kinds of demands for very long. The rules are in place so we can serve the most families in our city. So, no," she decreed. "We can't go back to the old system." Megan didn't push any further, because she knew her friend well enough to realize that when Ashley had made up her mind, the discussion was closed. But Megan's heart just couldn't bear to let the matter end there.

Lest we doubt that Satan and his demons are always actively trying to sabotage the work of God through attacks such as the one Ashley and Megan experienced, let's reflect on the passage at the beginning of this chapter (read Ephesians 6:12–17 for the full picture). While both Ashley and Megan had heeded the warnings to expect spiritual attack as they opened the food pantry ministry, neither of the women anticipated the spiritual powers to attack their rock-solid friendship. But it happened.

As the days went on, Ashley noted with satisfaction that her new system was indeed successful and there was no more double or triple dipping into the limited food supplies. And, to her delight, they were able to go beyond the projected number of families being served each week. From a numbers standpoint, it was a win-win. However, Ashley also took note of Megan's lack of enthusiasm about these accomplishments. Megan became more and more distant when they talked. Ashley also began to notice that Megan didn't seem interested in serving in the food pantry any more than was absolutely necessary. *I'm determined to find a way through this impasse*, Ashley thought.

Our friendship is worth so much more than a disagreement about how we can best serve our community.

Finally, unable to stand the chilly atmosphere in their friendship, Ashley invited Megan over for coffee and conversation. She brewed Megan's coffee of choice and ordered her favorite pastry from a nearby bakery. "Please, Lord," she prayed, "help me to be quiet and truly hear what Megan has to say. Help me to see this situation from her perspective, and give us wisdom on how to move forward."

Take-away Action Thought

When my friend and I have a disagreement, I will pray for the self-control to quietly listen to what my friend is saying and why. I will ask God for wisdom and insight to help us work through whatever issue is coming between us. If I'm able, I will gladly defer to my friend's preferences in the matter.

My Heart's Cry to You, O Lord

Father, I am truly heartbroken over the impasse my friend and I are experiencing. I know that in our heart of hearts we both want what is best in this situation. The problem is that we're coming at it from different perspectives. I'm thankful that both of us are your children and that we're earnestly praying for your will. Give us your wisdom to see that the spiritual forces of darkness would love nothing better than for us to give way to anger, impatience, and pride. Help us to honor you by not demanding our own way but rather humbly seeking your will in this situation. Amen.

Finding Joyful Freedom in Self-Forgetfulness

1. Self-forgetfulness with others. "For our struggle is not against flesh and blood, but against rulers, against the authorities, against the powers of this dark world." If I find myself at an impasse with a friend, I will spend time praying for God to give me his wisdom and insight on how to work through this issue. I will gladly defer to my friend's preferences if at all possible, knowing that dark spiritual forces want to "steal and kill and destroy" all that is good and honoring to God (John 10:10).

2. Self-forgetfulness in me. "Put on the full armor of God, so that when the day of evil comes, you may be able to stand your ground." Each morning this week, I will figuratively put on the full armor of God so that I am spiritually, mentally, and emotionally prepared to fight against the spiritual forces that will come against me as I seek to honor and serve the Lord each day.

3. Self-forgetfulness with God. "Take up the shield of faith, with which you can extinguish all the flaming arrows of the evil one." Since I know believers will fight one spiritual battle after another, I need to be a good remember-er. To help me remember how God has provided for me, I will keep a record of these wonderful accounts. If I haven't already started, I will begin a journal and make note of the how, when, and where of what occurred and how God faithfully supplied my every need.

Chapter 14

Self-Forgetfulness – With Our Acquaintances

But now in Christ Jesus you who once were far away have
been brought near by the blood of Christ. For he himself
is our peace, who has made the two groups one and
has destroyed the barrier, the dividing wall of hostility.
. . . He came and preached peace to you who were far
away and peace to those who were near. For through
him we both have access to the Father by one Spirit.

Ephesians 2:13–14, 17–18

*This is the good news of the gospel. Peace came. Peace
lived. Peace died. Peace rose again. Peace reigns on your
behalf. Peace indwells you by the Spirit. Peace graces you
with everything you need. Peace convicts, forgives, and
delivers you. Peace will finish his work in you. Peace will
welcome you into glory, where Peace will live with you in
peace and righteousness forever. Peace isn't a faded dream.
No, Peace is real. Peace is a person, and his name is Jesus.*

Paul David Tripp

A s a lover of parties, Hannah was looking forward to spending an afternoon planning the end-of-year celebration for her son's class. She was also equally excited about sharing the afternoon with her best friend Joy. Eight months pregnant and feeling more than ready to give birth to her third child, Hannah was simply feeling her feels in big ways these days.

Gathering her supplies and list of ideas, Hannah texted Joy: "Heading your way. Be there in 20." Within seconds, she received a reply: "Great. FYI, slight change of plans. Courtney offered to help us plan the party. Didn't know how to say no. Sorry."

Hannah exhaled a big sigh of disappointment along with no small measure of irritation. "Really? Lord, really?" she groused silently. "I was so looking forward to spending time alone with my best friend and now everything has changed. I can't believe we have to work with Courtney, either. She's unreliable, and she's proven that every time she signs up for the volunteer parent jobs at the school. And, honestly, Courtney is hard to get along with—and everyone knows it."

Hannah sat down at her kitchen table and stared at her phone. "I need to respond to Joy in a positive way. I know my friend. I know she didn't intend for this to happen, and it's not her fault. And, to be honest, I think this might be our opportunity to share our love of Jesus with Courtney. Forgive me, Lord, for making this all about me."

Closing her eyes and taking a deep breath, Hannah tried to quiet her thoughts and emotions. "Jesus," she prayed, "please help me to let go of my plans for this afternoon and accept your plan with good grace. I really did want to spend some alone time with my dearest friend, and I'm disappointed. But I know you always have something good happening behind the scenes. Give me your grace and a humble servant's heart that's ready to love and serve today, no matter what that looks like. Help me to live the remainder of this day intentionally self-forgetful, for my good and your glory."

As Paul Tripp said, "Peace is a person, and his name is Jesus." And this peace, this person, Jesus, is the only one who can enable us to break down the walls of hostility and bring the hope of reconciliation to those God places on our paths. While believers may embrace this principle in theory, it's a lot more challenging to pursue this peace when we're asked to let go of our plans, preferences, hopes, and desires. Right?

When the plans we make for ourselves shift and shake, we sometimes react no differently than Hannah. Disappointed. Irritated. Feeling our feelings in big ways even when we aren't expecting a baby. All the emotions can come crashing down around us, taking us captive along the way if we aren't on our guard. Which is why living an intentionally self-forgetful life means having a day-to-day attitude of inner preparedness.

Each day, we must diligently schedule time to spend in our Father's presence, allowing ourselves to be renewed by reading his word and prayerfully readying ourselves for the day's responsibilities—whatever may come our way. Perhaps the "amen" to gaining inner preparedness is to conclude our time with God by ending our prayers with "If the Lord wills" or "Your will be done." In either case, we need to acknowledge with both our attitude and our words that, despite our best-laid plans, God's will and God's way must reign supreme over our own. May this peace in the person of Jesus rule within our hearts so that we don't skip a beat when our plans change and we're called on to defer to someone else. May we gladly submit to God's perfect plans so we can be part of his greater eternal purpose.

Take-away Action Thought

When I'm forced to abandon my plans for the day, I won't complain. Instead, I will learn to accept these unexpected changes as part of God's perfect and greater purpose for both myself and those I'm called to love and serve.

My Heart's Cry to You, O Lord

Father, I need to ask for your forgiveness. When my plans suddenly changed, I was naturally disappointed and even irritated. I was looking forward to spending time doing what I wanted. I felt like I deserved and needed this time. But I have to let go of my disappointment and step back to see the bigger picture of what's happening here. Because I believe you are in the business of divine interruptions and divine orchestrations, I know that I can trust you to transform what may seem like a difficult appointment into something eternally meaningful. Help me to be inwardly prepared to live an intentionally self-forgetful life by embracing this closing to every one of my prayers: "Thy will be done." Amen.

Finding Joyful Freedom in Self-Forgetfulness

1. Self-forgetfulness with others. "He came and preached peace to you who were far away and peace to those who were near." Each day this week, I will pray for those acquaintances of mine I struggle to understand or relate to in meaningful ways. I will pray for each person and ask God to help me to see them the same way he

75

sees them. I will look for the good and then share these positive insights the next time I see them.

2. Self-forgetfulness in me. "For he himself is our peace, who has made the two groups one and has destroyed the barrier, the dividing wall of hostility." I will ask the Lord to reveal to me if I'm harboring an unloving attitude toward anyone. If I am, then I will ask for God's forgiveness and look for practical ways to show love toward these individuals.

3. Self-forgetfulness with God. "For through him we both have access to the Father by one Spirit." Each evening, I'll take time to reflect on the interactions I had with various people. I'll pray with a mindful awareness toward noticing how selfless my walk and my talk were during that day. I'll make sure my attitude is right before the Lord and confess my sins as needed.

Chapter 15

How Self-Forgetfulness Changes Us

Be filled with the Spirit, speaking to one another with psalms,
hymns, and songs from the Spirit. Sing and make music
from your heart to the Lord, always giving thanks to God the
Father for everything, in the name of our Lord Jesus Christ.

Ephesians 5:18–20

*People who draw a blank when asked what they're grateful
for—after running through the fairly automatic litany
of faith and family and food and health—can never be
those who draw nearest to God, not when He has given us
so many ways to answer this simple question. . . . People
who remember to thank God for everything from pliers and
pruners to paper plates are people who know what "everything"
is all about. And why shouldn't that person be you?*

Nancy Leigh DeMoss

A few weeks ago, remembering to say "thank you" for "everything" was put to the test. It began as a typical Sunday for our family. After our church service, we visited my parents and were planning to sit down to eat together when my daughter pulled me aside and told me about the severe pain that she was having—which was only getting worse. After hearing her description, I realized she was passing a kidney stone. Within minutes we were headed to the closest emergency room. While in reality it only took us about fifteen minutes to get there, those were some of the longest minutes of my life. When my four children were very young, I began to develop kidney stones on a regular basis. I thank the Lord I haven't suffered from one in many years due to modern medicine, but the recollection of that past horrendous·pain is never far from my memory. Those long-ago, middle-of-the-night trips to the ER remain lodged firmly in the recesses of my mind. To this day, it only takes someone describing their own kidney stone history for me to shudder, literally.

As I drove my daughter to the ER that Sunday morning, I heard her shallow breathing as she prayed in between groans for grace and strength, while rocking back and forth in agony. Truthfully, I wanted to be anywhere except in that car right then. I knew exactly what she was going through, and it was almost unbearable to hear her cries for help and be unable to do anything about it.

Yet, despite the mental and emotional trauma I experienced as I watched my daughter suffer, I sensed another stronger, faith-driven voice fill my heart and mind. I began silently thanking God for every specific blessing I could think of that day. I thanked him that we lived close to medical care and that we had insurance. I thanked him that, although it was winter in Michigan, today the roads were clear of snow and ice. I thanked him that because I knew exactly what was happening to my child, I could advocate for her better than anyone else in our family. I thanked him that I could assure her that her pain would end.

Though her restless movements and cries to God didn't cease when we arrived at the hospital, I felt myself calming down and focusing on what was most needed. If ever there was a time for me to embrace a self-forgetful attitude so I could help someone else, this was it. God gave me what I needed to get my daughter the help she needed. And I thank him for that.

Saying thank you to God for everything? How does that work? How can anyone give thanks when the worst is unfolding all around them? God's word is filled with many passages about the need to embrace an attitude of humble gratefulness that trusts in God's timing and plans more than we trust in our own.

As God's beloved children, we must prioritize spending time getting to know who our God is by studying Scripture, meditating on it, and memorizing it. I am fully aware that if I hadn't been in my own church service that fateful morning and listened to God's truth faithfully expounded, my own perspective and attitude may well have been different during that car ride to the hospital. But God knew how my day was going to transpire. He knew what I would need to love and serve my daughter. God prepared my heart and mind in advance through the hearing of his word, corporate worship, and prayer.

In reflection, I can see his faithful hand on everything from the last-minute decision to visit my parents, where we would all be together, to the clear roads and the empty ER waiting area where my daughter found immediate care. As difficult as it was to witness her suffering up close and personal, it was exactly where I needed to be. As I drove to the ER admissions, I prayed for grace and strength for her while she suffered. I prayed for God's favor and mercies to surround us both once we entered the hospital. Then, by faith, I began thanking him for the already obvious mercies he had orchestrated.

Perhaps another lesson learned was this: Because I was forced to witness the pain my daughter was suffering, I grew a little braver. For years, I've avoided discussing the topic of kidney stones because it was such an awful season of living in fear for me, and it took me a long time to work through a rising panic whenever I felt a pain in my back. Yes, PTSD (post-traumatic stress disorder) might well apply here in relation to kidney stone sufferers. But in his divine providence, God helped change me by giving me the grace to face my fear. And in doing so, I learned to trust him more by taking those much-needed self-forgetful steps, even though it caused me temporary emotional distress. God was there with me, and he was with my daughter. What is even more astounding to me is that God was there ahead of time, preparing us for what we were going to face! And I thank him for that.

Take-away Action Thought

In those painful moments when I need to push past my own emotional and spiritual discomfort, I will stand firm on God's promises to provide for my every need. I will, by faith, begin thanking him for those powerful truths.

My Heart's Cry to You, O Lord

Father, I stand in the need of prayer. I am facing a personally troubling scenario that I've often attempted to push out of my mind and my memory. Yet today, I am forced to confront my old fears, and I so need your grace and strength. Help me, by faith, to begin thanking you for every mercy, every blessing, and every good thing, right here and now. I know that when I choose to focus on you and your faithful love for me, everything inside of my heart and mind shifts to a peaceful and calm place. I want to honor you by trusting you today. You are worthy of my trust in every situation, and I am grateful my heart knows that to be true. Amen.

Finding Joyful Freedom in Self-forgetfulness

1. Self-forgetfulness with others. "Be filled with the Spirit, speaking to one another with psalms, hymns, and songs from the Spirit." This week, when I am in a position to be an encouragement to others, I will purposefully do so. I will make sure I speak out loud about the mercies and blessings of God, and I will share that truth to build the faith of my friends and family.

2. Self-forgetfulness in me. "Sing and make music from your heart to the Lord." Every day this week, whenever I'm in the car or at home, I will turn on worship music and sing along. I'll pay attention to how my attitude and heart lift after focusing on praising God through song each day.

3. Self-forgetfulness with God. "Always [give] thanks to God the Father for everything, in the name of our Lord Jesus Christ." As I journal each day, I will write down at least five mercies and blessings from God. I will thoughtfully include even those difficult, character-stretching scenarios that at first glance don't seem like blessings.

Chapter 16

How Self-Forgetfulness Matures Us

Love must be sincere. Hate what is evil; cling to what is good. Be devoted to one another in love. Honor one another above yourselves. Never be lacking in zeal, but keep your spiritual fervor, serving the Lord. Be joyful in hope, patient in affliction, faithful in prayer. Share with the Lord's people who are in need. Practice hospitality.

Romans 12:9–13

Your worries are taking you away from the present, where God is at work. Perhaps you think that God will not be with you tomorrow. . . . Not true. He will give you power for right now. He is doing something right now. In the midst of chaos, the Spirit often gives us a simple and clear mission, such as choosing to trust in God's love, listening to another person, helping someone in his or her need, or preparing lunch. Your God has made you a partner in bringing his kingdom to earth. Look around to see what he is doing and how he might want you to participate with him.

Edward Welch

Becca gazed around her house, making sure everything was in its place. As she walked from room to room, she mentally checked off everything she needed for her guests' arrival. Bedroom made up with clean sheets and welcome baskets of assorted snacks and personal care items? Check. Bathrooms scrubbed, scoured, and shining? Check. Kitchen cleaned and stocked with a variety of food and drink? Check. Living room swept and dusted, and fresh flowers placed on the tables? Check. Becca sighed deeply. *I'm as ready as I can be*, she reassured herself. *I've made list after list of every possible need and want my guests might have. But the rub is this: I've never met this couple before, so I can't be completely sure I'm ready.*

Becca took another turn around each room and shuddered, as if that simple physical exercise could rid her of the anxiety she was feeling inside. Then she realized she'd better start on dinner while she had the time. Marching into her spotless kitchen, she began pulling out the ingredients for a simple supper of soup, freshly baked bread, and salad. *I do hope they like this recipe*, she worried. *Everyone else seems to—but again, I've never met this missionary couple. How could I even guess what they may like or not like? Pastor told me not to worry, but that is easier said than done!*

Never in a million years would Becca have expected to open up her home to visiting missionaries from her church district. *But I shouldn't have been so surprised when Pastor asked me if I was open to the idea. I'm alone now. I have the space. I enjoy having friends over for a meal. But this? This is hospitality on a much bigger scale. I rarely host overnight guests. And I have certainly never entertained complete strangers.*

Becca realized there was only one person who could truly understand how she was feeling. "Lord," she prayed, "I really believe you want me to do this. I just wish I wasn't so nervous.

Help me to take a deep breath and exhale all my worries and fears." Closing her eyes, she did just that. She breathed in and then exhaled out much of her tension. *Okay, now back to work. It wouldn't do to not have a meal hot and ready when they arrive!*

The beauty of a self-forgetful heart is that it's characterized by sincere devotion to honor others' needs above one's own. The self-forgetful heart is determined—even in the midst of personal insecurities, doubts, overthinking—to look for ways to love, serve, and practice hospitality. Becca certainly did marvelous work preparing her home for the traveling missionary couple who would be staying with her for a few days. Attentive to every detail, her home was indeed a haven of rest and rejuvenation for anyone who was blessed to be her guest.

And yet, despite all of Becca's outward preparations, isn't it somewhat paradoxical how nervous and worried she felt on the inside? An outsider would probably assume she was as put together inside as her beautiful home was on the outside. But she wasn't. Like so many of us, she had her moments of doubts and even regrets about saying yes to this ministry of hospitality. She had felt the Spirit's nudge to accept this assignment with a glad and ready heart. But as the time to actually serve others drew nearer, she became nervous about it.

Perhaps the most significant spiritual truth found in the passage from Romans at the beginning of this chapter is this admonition from the Lord to us, his beloved children and servants: "Honor one another above yourselves. Never be lacking in zeal, but keep your spiritual fervor, serving the Lord. Be joyful in hope, patient in affliction, faithful in prayer." It's the Lord's personal message to each of us to live and serve others with a self-forgetful attitude. These are the ABCs of serving self-forgetfully, even when our hearts may tremble inside with the magnitude of what God has called us to do:

Honor others above ourselves—put their welfare first and above our own personal discomfort.

Serve the Lord by serving others with enthusiasm.

Faithfully commit our service to prayer and exude a joyful, hopeful spirit even when things don't go as expected.

Remember that we serve for three reasons: (1) Jesus saved us, (2) Jesus promised to be with us, and (3) Jesus goes before us.

 Take-away Action Thought

Whenever I enter into a new area of service, I'll remind myself that I may experience moments of doubt and worry. When these anxious feelings begin to stir within me, I'll take pen to paper and list all the wondrous ways God prepared me, guided me, and led me to this place of service. I will say a prayer of thanks for the opportunity to serve others using whatever resources God has blessed me with.

My Heart's Cry to You, O Lord

Father, I remember how excited I was when I said an enthusiastic yes to this ministry opportunity. I was so grateful I was being given this chance to use the many resources you've given me to bless others. Why am I then so surprised by these sudden feelings of doubt and worry? I guess I'm scared that I'm not talented, smart, or gifted enough to make a difference. Please help me to remember that it doesn't matter if I'm not enough, because I rely on your strength, grace, and power to serve. I know that perfection is an unrealistic and unhealthy expectation I will never live up to. Help me instead to focus on doing my best and then leave the results in your faithful hands. Give me a self-forgetful attitude so I can wholeheartedly serve those you bring my way. Amen.

Finding Joyful Freedom in Self-Forgetfulness

1. Self-forgetfulness with others. "Be devoted to one another in love." During the upcoming week, I will spend time preparing for my work of ministry. I'll make detailed lists of what I need to best serve those God brings my way. I will design my plans to fit the unique needs and preferences of these individuals.

2. Self-forgetfulness in me. "Honor one another above yourselves." I'll spend time this week searching for Scripture verses I can refer to when I begin to doubt my decision to serve in this new ministry. I will write out as many of these verses as I can find in the Bible and keep them nearby for easy reference day and night.

3. Self-forgetfulness with God. "Be joyful in hope, patient in affliction, faithful in prayer." As I begin this new chapter in my life, I'll make time daily to pray for this ministry and keep an up-to-date journal on all the happenings. This will enable me to both pray for current needs and give thanks to God for his faithfulness in providing for my needs as I seek to meet the needs of others.

Chapter 17

How Self-Forgetfulness Humbles Us

May God himself, the God of peace, sanctify you through
and through. May your whole spirit, soul, and body be
kept blameless at the coming of our Lord Jesus Christ.
The one who calls you is faithful, and he will do it.

1 Thessalonians 5:23–24

*We begin to pout, become irritated with God, and then
say, "Oh well, I can't help it. I prayed and things didn't
turn out right anyway. So I'm simply going to give up on
everything." Just think what would happen if we acted
like this in any other area of our lives? Am I fully prepared
to allow God to grip me by His power and do a work in
me that is truly worthy of Himself? Sanctification is not
my idea of what I want God to do for me—sanctification
is God's idea of what He wants to do for me. But He has
to get me into the state of mind and spirit where I will
allow Him to sanctify me completely, whatever the cost.*

Oswald Chambers

Kelsey was busy setting up the spare bedroom for her mother-in-law's upcoming visit. As she remade the bed with fresh sheets, she looked around the room, trying to decide if her mother-in-law would require an extra comforter. *These days, Helen is cold most of the time,* Kelsey thought. *I want her to be as comfortable as she can.* Once she was satisfied with her preparations, her next task was to plan a nutritious menu for Helen and their family. *I know she doesn't eat as much as she should. She eats like a bird! But I'm determined to help her put on a few pounds while she's with us.*

Kelsey smiled. She cherished her husband's mother and wanted her to live healthily for as long as possible before God called her home. She was jotting down possible dinner selections when Jack walked in. "Hey there! Busy day?" he asked his wife as he snuck a peek at her list.

"I've been busy, but this is the last task on my to-do list," Kelsey answered happily. "One thing—a senior retirement home called today. They have an opening next month. I have to be honest, Jack, I was shocked to receive that call. I thought we agreed to consider having your mom move in here with us when the time came for assisted living."

"No, we didn't agree," her husband said gently. "It was your idea to have Mom move in here with us. I think she would be much happier with her own space and her privacy. We can visit her as often as we want, remember. Mom doesn't want us micromanaging her every move. You know how you get when she visits. You hover over her like she's a child."

Kelsey felt stunned by his kind but honest words. Did her mother-in-law truly feel the way Jack had just described—smothered by Kelsey's attention and love? To be truthful, Kelsey felt like she had been slapped by Jack's words. She was thankful when he left the kitchen to change his clothes before dinner.

"Lord, I feel so misunderstood and hurt," she prayed. "Is Jack right? Does my mother-in-law really feel like I'm treating her like a child when she visits? You know how much I love her. I'm only trying to do what's best for her. I've never tried to make Helen bend to my will. Help me to accept this uncomfortable truth graciously. I need to rethink how I approach her needs as well as her wants. Maybe I have been unintentionally assertive about trying to force her to take better care of herself. Oh dear. If my husband's right, then I need to apologize to Helen and the sooner the better. Help me, Lord, to put aside what I think is best and pray about what's truly best for Helen."

Ouch, right? Few things are as painful as the emotional hurt we feel after we have done our best to care for another person, only to discover that our best intentions perhaps weren't the best after all. It's hard to accept the realization that maybe, just maybe, we have been manipulating circumstances and settings in such a way as to nudge our loved one toward what we consider is best. Like many of us, Kelsey hadn't a clue that all her caregiving and hospitable acts of service weren't appreciated in the way she hoped.

Like Kelsey, I've been in the position of trying to arrange and rearrange people, places, and things for the benefit of everyone involved. And, like Kelsey, I've felt the sting of regret when I realized I wasn't being as sensitive as I had imagined. Had I been determined to get my own way? No, but I wasn't exactly on top of my self-forgetfulness game either. I had assumed that my preferences would mirror my family's preferences—until I realized they didn't. Then I needed to rethink my presuppositions and go ask others what they most wanted and needed. I had to let go of what I wanted them to want! Self-forgetfulness includes graciously bestowing on others what is best for them—not what we believe is best for them. That's a big difference.

In order to let go of our perfectly laid plans, we need to allow God to have his perfect way in us. We have to exercise self-control to let go of needing to do things our way. Especially when the Lord is directing us to serve others according to their needs, not our whims and wishes. We must surrender our own wishes and embrace the self-forgetfulness that goes along with truly loving our family, friends, and neighbors as they most want to be loved.

Take-away Action Thought

When I am trying to serve others, I will be sure to ask them what they need and want most. I will not presume to know what is best for them.

My Heart's Cry to You, O Lord

Father, I honestly had the best intentions today. I believed I knew what was best for my loved one. I only wanted what would help her to be comfortable and feel loved. But I failed to ask her about what she most wanted and needed from me. Oh Lord, I need to learn to pray first, then ask questions, and make my plans accordingly. Help me to not forget that as I embrace a humble, self-forgetful attitude in life, I also need to graciously give way to others' preferences over my own. Amen.

Finding Joyful Freedom in Self-Forgetfulness

1. Self-forgetfulness with others. "May your whole spirit, soul, and body be kept blameless." I will revisit recent events and consider whether or not I've exhibited humble self-forgetfulness when I served others around me. Why or why not? Do I need to approach serving others differently?

2. Self-forgetfulness in me. "May God himself, the God of peace, sanctify you through and through." I will spend time praying for the Lord to reveal to me if I've been selfish in my heart attitude toward others. If the Lord brings to mind specific instances when I have prioritized my preferences over others' wants and desires, then I'll make reparations as needed.

3. Self-forgetfulness with God. "The one who calls you is faithful, and he will do it." Knowing that God desires to do an ongoing work of sanctification within me, I will ask him to show me where I need to stretch and grow in his grace. I will write down my thoughts and intentions in my journal as a reminder of the spiritual journey I'm on.

Chapter 18

How Self-Forgetfulness Challenges Us

Therefore if you have any encouragement from being
united with Christ, if any comfort from his love, if any
common sharing in the Spirit, if any tenderness and
compassion, then make my joy complete by being
like-minded, having the same love, being one in spirit
and of one mind. Do nothing out of selfish ambition
or vain conceit. Rather, in humility value others above
yourselves, not looking to your own interests but each of
you to the interests of others. In your relationships with
one another, have the same mindset as Christ Jesus.

Philippians 2:1–5

*The chief motivation behind Paul's service was not love
for others but love for his Lord. If our devotion is to the
cause of humanity, we will be quickly defeated and
brokenhearted, since we will often be confronted with a
great deal of ingratitude from other people. But if we are
motivated by our love for God, no amount of ingratitude
will be able to hinder us from serving one another.*

Oswald Chambers

Greg and his brother Grant ran a campground with a small but growing water park attached. Every winter when campers were scarce, the brothers set about planning another expansion to their already impressive layout. Together, they studied all the options open to them for expanding their little camping community, mindful about the most efficient ways to keep the costs down.

Greg, the elder brother and a committed Christian, ran the day-to-day operation of the campsite while keeping close oversight on the bottom-line finances. He learned from his own father that it's all well and good to open a business, but to keep it solvent, someone has to take on the fiscal responsibility and make sure there is accountability for every dollar spent. His younger brother, Grant, was the assistant manager. Grant leaned heavily on his charismatic personality as he half-heartedly muddled through his daily responsibilities with a lackadaisical attitude. From Grant's perspective, if someone wasn't screaming "Fire!" then there was no need to rush—or to work, for that matter.

With their differing approaches to work in the family business, the two brothers often found themselves at odds with each other. It wasn't uncommon for Greg to find himself clenching his teeth as he tried to maintain an outer calm while his insides were roiling whenever Grant showed up late for work or was found wasting time playing games on his computer.

Greg had tried time and again to talk to his brother about the need for commitment and hard work if their campground was to remain successful. But Grant never really paid attention to Greg's warnings. Instead, Grant felt like Greg expected too much of him. Grant was not only lazy—he was self-centered.

What was Greg to do? It seemed like all his efforts to get Grant to take personal responsibility for his share of the work only fell on deaf ears. Then one day, after another particularly challenging conversation about working Saturdays until the winter cleanup was complete, Greg sat down defeated and discouraged. "Lord," Greg prayed, "please give me the wisdom and understanding I need to make this campground a success. I really don't know how I can continue trying to do my own work in addition to Grant's. I need help figuring out how to handle this situation." Head in his hands, Greg sat silently waiting for some fresh resolution to come to mind. Then the phone rang. "Hello?"

"Greg, this is Matt," said the person on the other end of the line. "You've been on my mind all day. Can you drop over after work and have dinner with us?"

Greg shook his head in amazement and looked upward. "Yes, Lord, I'm hearing you." Greg accepted the invitation with thanks and spent the remainder of the afternoon in wonder at God's always perfect timing and provision. "Only God would orchestrate a phone call and a dinner invitation from one of the most successful businessmen in town."

"If our devotion is to the cause of humanity, we will be quickly defeated and brokenhearted." *But*, "if we are motivated by our love for God, no amount of ingratitude will be able to hinder us from serving one another." This Oswald Chambers insight is spot on as we strive to love others from a purely self-forgetful perspective. We must be willing to be unappreciated, misunderstood, and taken for granted if we are to honor God's plan and remain committed to others.

The golden standard is this: If I'm more concerned about loving you from a pure heart, then I will intentionally love you, keep communicating with you, and continue to build bridges toward you no matter how challenging it may be to do so. I will find my comfort and consolation in the Lord even when you fail to live up to my desires and expectations.

Greg did all he could to love his brother Grant and to help him take personal responsibility for his attitude and work. But Grant viewed his brother as someone who only got in the way of what he wanted: little work and lots of leisure time. And this is the point where the problem originated between the two brothers.

Grant had two options when it came to Greg standing in the way of what he wanted: He could either get angry at him, or he could confess his failings and reconcile with his brother. Grant wasn't yet willing to acknowledge his mistakes and misguided priorities, though, thus the impasse.

Still, Greg held out hope. He took his burden about Grant to God in prayer and asked for wisdom, insight, and guidance. And as Greg sought the Lord's counsel, God creatively answered by sending him help from a Christian businessman who had many years of experience working through employee standoffs and resistant workers with lousy work ethics.

However, while Greg would gain terrific counsel from Matt that evening about how to work with Grant, he would never forget Matt's most important (albeit challenging) advice: "No matter how many times your brother falters and fails at work, never give up on him as a person. Keep loving him. Keep investing in him as a man." Greg determined to do just that.

Take-away Action Thought

If I find myself struggling to love and invest in another person who is resistant to everything I say and do, I will take an introspective look at how I'm communicating with this individual. I will ask the Lord to reveal to me any resentment I may be harboring against them that may be coming in between us.

My Heart's Cry to You, O Lord

Father, I need your grace and strength right now. I feel like giving up on this challenging person in my life. I have tried and tried to love him. I have worked hard to invest in his life for his good. But it seems like no matter what approach I take, it never yields any lasting results. From my perspective, it feels like the walls between us are growing thicker by the day. Help me to not harbor any bitterness or resentment against him. Instead, give me an ever-growing desire to love him well. Above all, I want my loved one to come to a saving faith in you, Lord. Give me your words, I pray. Amen.

Finding Joyful Freedom in Self-Forgetfulness

1. Self-forgetfulness with others. "In humility value others above yourselves, not looking to your own interests but each of you to the interests of others." Each day this week, I'll spend a few minutes prayerfully reflecting on the most pressing needs of those around me. If the Lord brings specific wants and needs to my mind, I'll do my best to meet them.

2. Self-forgetfulness in me. "Do nothing out of selfish ambition or vain conceit." During my daily quiet times, I'll reflect on the day's conversations. I'll take note of any unkind, impatient, or irritable words that passed between me and others. If I communicated in a way that didn't honor the Lord, I will swiftly seek forgiveness.

3. Self-forgetfulness with God. "In your relationships with one another, have the same mindset as Christ Jesus." Knowing that Jesus gave his life on the cross and poured himself out for others, I will ask the Lord to create in me that same willing desire to be poured out for the well-being and benefit of others. Then I'll make notes in my journal as I witness how God begins to answer that worthy prayer.

Chapter 19

How Self-Forgetfulness Encourages Us

Godly sorrow brings repentance that leads to salvation and leaves no regret, but worldly sorrow brings death. See what this godly sorrow has produced in you: what earnestness, what eagerness to clear yourselves, what indignation, what alarm, what longing, what concern, what readiness to see justice done. At every point you have proved yourselves to be innocent in this matter. By all this we are encouraged.

2 Corinthians 7:10–11, 13

O my Saviour, Help me. I am so slow to learn, so prone to forget, so weak to climb; I am in the foothills when I should be on the heights; I am pained by my graceless heart, my prayerless days, my poverty of love, my sloth in the heavenly race, my sullied conscience, my wasted hours, my unspent opportunities. I am blind while light shines around me: take the scales from my eyes, grind to dust the evil heart of unbelief. Give me increase and progress in grace so that there may be more decision in my character, more vigour in my purposes, more elevation in my life, more fervor in my devotion, more constancy in my zeal.

Puritan Prayer

Maggie was up early, drinking her first and best cup of coffee of the day while reading through her yearly Bible plan. She made notes as she read to remind herself to revisit some of the more difficult passages. Maggie was an early bird who loved this precious time alone with the Lord before the rest of the family got up and going. As she read, she heard her adult daughter Chelsea in the kitchen. Since she was hardly ever interrupted in the morning, though, she didn't pay much attention and returned to her study in the book of Ephesians.

Moments later, Chelsea plopped herself down on the recliner opposite her mom and declared, "I made a discovery about myself. I have autism spectrum disorder." Maggie then listened closely as Chelsea explained why she believed she had high-functioning autism. "What do you think, Mom?"

Maggie took a deep breath, said a quick silent prayer for wisdom, and answered, "Well, Chelsea, I agree with you. But I'm a little surprised by this sudden revelation of yours. Don't you remember your dad and me talking to you about this possibility over the years? We discussed it many times to help you better understand yourself."

After a few moments of lingering silence, Chelsea replied, nonplussed, "Nope, I must have blocked it out. I have no memory of you ever bringing this to my attention before." Getting to her feet, she left the room to get ready for work. From her point of view, the discussion was over.

Maggie, however, felt troubled, confused, and not a little discouraged. "Lord, I'm really shocked that Chelsea is only now realizing she has autism. I'm dumbfounded. And I feel like somewhere along the way I must have failed to communicate how this disorder may affect her. What happened, Lord? Am I not correctly remembering the discussions we had with

Chelsea from middle school on? Somewhere along the way, the message got lost, dismissed, or ignored. Help me, Lord, I'm at a loss."

If you've ever been part of a conversation where you assumed you and a loved one were on the same page regarding a specific issue and then discovered you weren't, you know exactly how Maggie felt after Chelsea made her stunning self-revelatory announcement. Quite honestly, she was flabbergasted. The more she turned the conversation over in her own mind, the more discouraged she felt. But at precisely that juncture, God stepped in and began a new work of deepening and maturing Maggie to be even more fit for his kingdom service.

After taking time to revisit the past conversations Maggie remembered quite clearly, she realized that even though her now-grown daughter might recall the past differently, it was today that mattered. True, she felt confused about how her child might have totally dismissed those important parent-to-child discussions. But, she realized, perhaps Chelsea wasn't ready to receive this particular insight about herself until now. Maggie knew that God is the sovereign ruler and orchestrator of his children's lives. Perhaps God had guarded Chelsea's mind from thinking too much about having this disorder as a teen because she had not been ready to hear it.

Maggie's current challenge was to embrace a humble, self-forgetful posture. At the outset, when Chelsea began to share her newfound revelation, Maggie was tempted to jump in and interrupt her daughter with reminders of past conversations. She wanted to reassure her that she had not missed the signs, been inattentive, or slipped up as a mom. But having just spent time in God's word, Maggie realized that something far more important was happening. *I don't need to prove to Chelsea I was right all those years ago. I don't need to convince myself that I've been a good mom, either. What I need to focus on is that God is doing his own good work in my daughter's life. I must rejoice in that truth because that encourages me. And that is enough. It has to be.*

Take-away Action Thought

When I'm blindsided by a conversation that tempts me to react defensively, I will pray and ask God for the self-control to be quiet so that I can really hear what the other person is telling me. If I'm troubled by what they say, I won't react. Instead, I'll take time to pray and think through what I've heard before I respond.

My Heart's Cry to You, O Lord

Father, I listened to my dear child share a personal revelation she has only just discovered about herself, something we've talked about many times through the years, and I'm confused. I don't understand my own troubled reaction, other than feeling I needed to clarify the facts of the past to defend my parenting. Lord, I was so discouraged. Then, after I took a little time alone and thought it through, I saw the bigger eternal picture. Now I'm encouraged. Thank you for helping me to embrace this self-forgetful posture in every area of my life—past and present. It's setting me joyfully free. Amen.

Finding Joyful Freedom in Self-Forgetfulness

1. Self-forgetfulness with others. "Godly sorrow brings repentance that leads to salvation and leaves no regret." This week I will be determined to be mindful of my attitudes and responses toward others as we interact and converse together. I will be more intentional about honing a humble, self-forgetful posture with every conversation I'm a part of.

2. Self-forgetfulness in me. "See what this godly sorrow has produced in you." During my daily quiet time with God, I will spend a few moments revisiting interactions with others in which I felt a need to defend myself, explain my actions, or correct others' interpretations of past events. I will not be discouraged by differing perspectives or comments. Instead, I will thank God and be encouraged that he is always doing a good work in each of us.

3. Self-forgetfulness with God. "At every point you have proved yourselves to be innocent in this matter. By all this we are encouraged." At the end of each day, I will spend time talking to God about those I've conversed with on that particular day. I'll take their needs to my heavenly Father and intercede on their behalf. I want to spend more time praying for the needs of others instead of focusing solely on my own.

Chapter 20

How Self-Forgetfulness Stretches Us to Serve

Do everything without grumbling or arguing, so that you may become blameless and pure, children of God without fault in a warped and crooked generation. Then you will shine among them like stars in the sky as you hold firmly to the word of life. And then I will be able to boast on the day of Christ that I did not run or labor in vain. But even if I am being poured out like a drink offering on the sacrifice and service coming from your faith, I am glad and rejoice with all of you.

Philippians 2:14–17

For the believer, peace is not to be found in ease of life. Real peace is only ever found in the presence, power, and grace of the Savior, the King, the Lamb, the I am. That peace is yours even when the storms of life take you beyond your natural ability, wisdom, and strength. You can live with hope and courage in the middle of what once would have produced discouragement and fear because you know you are never alone. The I am inhabits all situations, relationships, and locations by his grace. He is in you. He is with you. He is for you. He is your hope.

Paul David Tripp

J enelle hurried down the main aisle of the auditorium, eyeing her ticket and glancing at the alphabetized rows. The closer she got to the front, the more pleased and excited she felt. *I'm so much nearer to the center stage than I expected,* she thought happily. *This is going to be wonderful.*

Stopping at her assigned row, Jenelle made her way to her seat, sat down, and began arranging her personal belongings around her. *We only get to attend this work seminar once a year, and I'm going to drink in every minute of each session. It's almost like a vacation for me, not having to wrestle with my HR cases for a few days.* She sighed in contentment.

Jenelle was reaching for her notepad and pen when she felt a hand on her shoulder. When she looked up, she couldn't believe her eyes. *No, it can't be. This isn't happening!* Jenelle thought frantically. Seated in the row behind her was Emily, the new intern in Jenelle's department—and one of the primary reasons she'd been counting down the days until she got to escape to this seminar. *I didn't know she was coming. And with hundreds of participants, Emily gets seated behind me? Lord, this isn't fair!* Jenelle groused inwardly.

Emily greeted Jenelle enthusiastically, noting the happy coincidence that they were seated so closely together for the next few days. "We can take our breaks together, and lunch too!" Emily exclaimed, without any consideration of Jenelle's plans or preferences. Instead of replying, Jenelle just offered a weak smile. As Emily settled herself in her seat, Jenelle's pleasant thoughts of anticipation sank into ones of bitter disappointment. *Give me a challenge, I'll conquer it. Give me a deadline, I'll meet it. Give me an impossible employee scenario and I'll . . .* Jenelle stopped herself short. "Oh, Lord. You do have a sense of humor. Of all the colleagues and associates I expected to see here and looked forward to seeing, Emily was not on my list. Help me, Lord, to submit to your will, your plan for these next three days. Amen."

I had to stifle a laugh when Jenelle shared her story with me about a past work seminar she was looking forward to as an escape from the stress a new intern in her office was causing. As one of her firm's HR directors, Jenelle had tried without success to utilize all of her considerable skills and experience to help train and instruct Emily in the methodology of human resources. Nothing had been easy. Eventually, Jenelle recommended that Emily not pursue a career in human resources, because she simply wasn't good with people. Any people! Jenelle had lost count of the hours she had labored to undo Emily's mistakes and misfires with fellow staff members and clients.

This was the source of Jenelle's understandable desire for this time away from the office, so that she could replenish and refresh herself while gaining new insights and information. Emily seemed to have a knack for depleting Jenelle's mental and emotional reserves on an hourly basis, five days a week! As Jenelle and I talked about her initial reaction to seeing Emily at the seminar, we both found ourselves commiserating over those challenging people God keeps persistently inserting into our lives. Like Jenelle, there have been situations when my heart cried out, "I am not strong enough to handle this person and their problems. I am not enough. Please send someone else!" More often than not, God places that particular person right next to me just as he seated Emily behind Jenelle. Divine appointment? I really cannot answer it any other way.

Just as Jenelle submitted to God's apparent will and plan for her days at the seminar, I have found myself praying for an attitude of conscious self-forgetfulness by purposefully abandoning my plans in favor of God's perfect plan. As I acknowledge my own weakness and lean on God's strength to serve, he supplies it. And, most important of all, in the words of the apostle Paul, "Even if I am being poured out like a drink offering on the sacrifice and service coming from your faith, I am glad and rejoice."

May we say no to grumbling or arguing, so that we may become blameless and pure children of God in a crooked and perverse generation! And when "the storms of life take you beyond your natural ability, wisdom, and strength," as Paul Tripp says in the quote above, God will give us peace, hope, and courage to serve with the strength he provides.

Take-away Action Thought

When I'm placed in a situation with a difficult person, I will focus on the good news that God will provide me with all I need to serve from a self-forgetful perspective. I won't grumble or complain about his plan for me. Instead, I'll give thanks that I can trust him with all my hours and days, and with every person who fills them.

My Heart's Cry to You, O Lord

Father, I am disappointed. You know how much I was looking forward to this time away for rest and rejuvenation. But then the very person who has been causing me so much distress sits down right next to me. I don't even have the words to describe my emotions. Please, help me right now to set aside my expectations and submit to your perfect plan for me. I need your grace and strength to let go of what I wanted and pursue your will for me. Help me to remember that you are the potter and I am the clay. Amen.

Finding Joyful Freedom in Self-Forgetfulness

1. Self-forgetfulness with others. "You will shine among them like stars in the sky as you hold firmly to the word of life." This week, I will pray daily for that difficult person God has placed in my life, trusting that as I lift her up in prayer, my heart will grow more invested in her welfare and soften toward her.

2. Self-forgetfulness in me. "Do everything without grumbling or arguing." If I'm tempted to grumble or argue with God or with others this week, about work or acts of service, I'll focus on the truth that God's perfect plan and will for my life is always best. I'll spend time reading Scripture passages that deal with God's sovereignty in the lives of his children.

3. Self-forgetfulness with God. "Even if I am being poured out like a drink offering on the sacrifice and service coming from your faith, I am glad." Each evening this week, I will focus on honing a heart of praise and thanksgiving. No matter what the circumstances, my heart will rest at peace knowing that God sees and understands the most profitable uses of my gifts and talents.

Chapter 21

Taking Self-Forgetfulness into Our Prayer Rooms

"Still others, like seed sown among thorns, hear the word;
but the worries of this life, the deceitfulness of wealth
and the desires for other things come in and choke the
word, making it unfruitful. Others, like seed sown on good
soil, hear the word, accept it, and produce a crop—some
thirty, some sixty, some a hundred times what was sown."

Mark 4:18–20

*Worries can leave you spiritually vulnerable. "The cares of
the world" are your worries. These are not potent enough to
drag you away from Jesus, but they can leave you stagnant
and unfruitful. Notice how our worries tend to imagine a
future without God in it. Without God we have to prepare
for those future threats on our own. Life gradually gets
smaller. Our mission to trust Jesus and love other people
gets temporarily lost amid our future preparations.*

Edward Welch

Nina had made a habit of setting aside an afternoon every January to plan out specific half-days each month over the new year for prayer and fasting. Once she penciled in these monthly half-days, she scheduled weekly hour-long appointments with God to intercede on behalf of everyone and everything she had written about in her journal for that month. Nina had followed this plan year after year. Of course, she didn't just confine her praying to these monthly and weekly appointments. She also got up an hour early every morning to spend time reading the Bible and several devotionals and, of course, to pray.

Everyone who knew Nina called her a woman of prayer. If she promised to pray, she followed through and prayed. In fact, all of Nina's friends and family called on her to pray for them whenever anything significant was going on in their lives. It was her joy and privilege to bring specific needs before the throne of grace each and every day.

And then, Nina lost her job at the hospital where she worked as an administrator. Without any warning, cuts were made across the board in management and her position was eliminated. She was devastated.

For the first time in her career of over twenty years, Nina felt out of control. The stability she had always enjoyed at the hospital had been erased like chalk on a chalkboard. She felt shocked and dismayed, to be sure. But her long habit of daily Bible reading and prayer helped her cope with this major life change. She prayed. And prayed. And prayed some more. She expected the Lord to open another door immediately. But he didn't. Nina grew worried and her prayers lost their usual focus and faith-filled persistence. She stopped interceding for others because her heart and mind were now fixated on her own employment troubles.

Nina felt herself sinking emotionally under the fear of permanent joblessness. She found herself so overwhelmed by her own stress that she was unable to concentrate on anyone else's struggles or needs. Thankfully, her older brother Nick entered into the equation. Nick began making frequent after-work stops at her house to talk. And then they would pray. After Nick brought prayer for Nina's needs directly to the throne of grace, she felt relaxed for the first time in weeks. His faithfulness as a brother and as a prayer warrior helped Nina regain her focus on her faithful God and his promised provision. Slowly, she was able to let go of her worries and start interceding for others again. Nina the prayer warrior was back!

Can't we all identify with Nina's struggle to take her very real needs to the throne of grace and leave them there? It's a battle to be sure. As Edward Welch states in the quote above, she found herself "spiritually vulnerable" because she was full of worry. Her long history of praying with intentional self-forgetfulness was derailed because she was fighting her own internal battle with fear and worry. Haven't we all experienced a similar paralyzed state when we feel out of control?

Nina found herself, as Welch writes, "imagining a future without God in it," and she did indeed end up feeling like she was on her own when it came to preparing for the future. When we succumb to a future without God in it, what happens next? "Life gradually gets smaller. Our mission to trust Jesus and love other people gets temporarily lost amid our future preparations." The truth is that we can find ourselves so afraid of what may come next that our prayers for others (and even for ourselves) are stymied.

God faithfully interceded on Nina's behalf by sending along her brother to support and encourage her, and he will do the same for me and for you. As I contemplated the lessons Nina learned on her journey from personal worry to perfect peace, I realized how important it is for all Christ-followers to surround themselves with robust, faithful, like-minded fellow believers who will support, encourage, and challenge them. None of us can be on top of our spiritual game all the time. We need our fellow believing brothers and sisters to remind us of God's past faithfulness so that we can rest securely in that truth. Self-forgetfulness in prayer requires a thankful heart that reflects on God's past, present, and future faithfulness to meet our needs, and a willingness to be cared for by others when we get lost in our own stress and worry. And what a beautiful place that is to be when we lean fully into the faithfulness of God.

Take-away Action Thought

When I'm battling my way through a loss or scary uncertainty, I will open my journal and begin reading of God's past faithfulness to me as a reminder of how he has always kept his promise to meet my every need. Then I will thank him and begin praying for others.

My Heart's Cry to You, O Lord

Father, I am having the hardest time concentrating during prayer. My thoughts keep wandering back and forth between my present need and the worry I feel. I intended to sit down and pray through my list of prayer requests for others today—needs that are heavy on my heart! But my mind was so full of my own worries and anxieties that I was unable to focus on anyone but myself. Please help me to reflect on your past faithfulness to me and to give you thanks for every provision. I know that as I redirect my thoughts to you, peace will come, and then I will be able to pray on behalf of others once again. Amen.

Finding Joyful Freedom in Self-Forgetfulness

1. Self-forgetfulness with others. "Others, like seed sown on good soil, hear the word, accept it, and produce a crop." This week, I will take my journal and Bible in hand, and no matter what is going on in my life or how distracted I may be, I will write down the names of people I'm praying for and then look up a specific Bible verse to pray for them. I will intercede through this list, depending on these verses to help me better communicate my prayers to God.

2. Self-forgetfulness in me. "The desires for other things come in and choke the word, making it unfruitful." Each morning this week, I will ask the Lord to show me if I'm worrying, and then ask him for the grace to cast all my cares on Jesus. I will sit silently in his presence, recounting the many evidences of his perfect provision for me and his past faithfulness.

3. Self-forgetfulness with God. "Others . . . produce a crop—some thirty, some sixty, some a hundred times what was sown." At the end of the week, I'll spend time meditating on my prayers from the past seven days. I'll reflect on how I'm handling my own problems. Am I worrying? Am I anxious or afraid? Am I taking every thought captive to Christ, or am I wallowing in my fear and forgetting God's promises? In short, I'll take stock of my prayer life and refocus as needed.

Chapter 22

Praying Big Self-Forgetful Prayers

Therefore, since we are surrounded by such a great cloud
of witnesses, let us throw off everything that hinders
and the sin that so easily entangles. And let us run with
perseverance the race marked out for us, fixing our eyes
on Jesus, the pioneer and perfecter of faith. For the
joy set before him he endured the cross, scorning its
shame, and sat down at the right hand of the throne of
God. Consider him who endured such opposition from
sinners, so that you will not grow weary and lose heart.

Hebrews 12:1–3

*Perseverance is the quality of character that enables one
to pursue a goal in spite of obstacles and difficulties. It is
one thing to simply bear up under adversity. This in itself
is commendable. But God calls us to do more than simply
bear the load of adversity. He calls us to persevere (to press
forward) in the face of it. The Christian life is meant to be
active, not passive. The Christian is called to pursue with
diligence the will of God. To do this requires perseverance.*

Jerry Bridges

Vivian hung up the phone after saying good-bye to her daughter Ellie, who had just tearfully described her teen son's latest brush with the authorities. "Ross did it again," Ellie had sobbed. "He broke another curfew with us, and the police picked him up at the park where he and his friends were trying to take apart the playground equipment. Why is he so rebellious? I thought we turned a corner after last summer. Ross has been so much better around us here at home. And now this? I don't know how to deal with it."

Vivian listened intently to her daughter's grief for her child. She longed to be with Ellie, to put her arms around her and reassure her that things would be all right. But would they? She really didn't know. But Vivian was confident that God did know. She had interceded on behalf of her beloved grandson since before he was born. Rarely had Vivian missed a single day to pray for him to come to a saving relationship with Jesus Christ.

Watching her grandson grow through the years, she tailor-made her prayers to Ross's changing personality and his increasing bent toward harmful attitudes and behaviors. She pored over Scripture and jotted down specific passages she wanted to make sure she prayed back to God. It wasn't that God needed reminding of his powerful promises. No, it was an exercise in reminding Vivian herself of God's promised provision—and it helped her to continue to pray big prayers for Ross, even when all outward evidence pointed to nothing changing in his heart and mind.

But Vivian understood something important about prayer. When we realize that God calls us to not "simply bear the load of adversity" in prayer but to "persevere (to press forward) in the face of it," then we move into the dynamic, active realm of praying with self-forgetfulness. Vivian would never stop praying big prayers for her grandson. She knew better. In fact, the more trouble Ross got into, the more Vivian redoubled her efforts in prayer for him. She fixed her eyes on Jesus and refused to grow weary or lose heart.

I applaud Vivian's commitment to interceding on behalf of her grandson, despite the absence of any evidence that her prayers were making even a minimal difference in Ross's heart and mind. Vivian fixed her eyes squarely on Jesus. She refused to give way to discouragement or despair. She would never go down the road of self-pity or self-doubt, wondering why her prayers weren't being answered in her time or in her way.

Instead, Vivian pressed forward in her prayers and actively interceded on behalf of her wayward grandson. Day by day, she came before the Lord, beseeching him to give Ross a seeking heart. She prayed that Ross would recognize that he was a sinner and that he needed a Savior. She prayed that the Lord would give Ross a hunger for truth and righteousness. She worked through pages of written prayers she had designed especially for her beloved grandson.

Whenever Vivian did feel briefly discouraged or doubt-ridden about her grandson's escalating sinful behavior and rebellious attitude, she took herself to the throne of grace and talked to God about what she was feeling. Then she meditated on passages of Scripture that always brought her comfort and hope.

Vivian had learned over the years and through many setbacks and hardships to be diligent in pressing forward in prayer, despite whatever was happening in the world around her. She understood that it doesn't matter how we feel—we pray anyway and we never stop praying. We choose to press through those moments when we aren't sure if our prayers are being heard, because God's word tells us he hears the prayers of his children and he is attentive to every one of them. We choose the path of praying big prayers on behalf of others, and we never stop.

 Take-away Action Thought

Despite the seeming lack of any outward answer to prayer, I will actively press forward and persevere in my prayers on behalf of those I have committed to intercede for. I won't give way to feelings of doubt or discouragement if the answers don't come when I hoped or as I had hoped. Instead, I will trust in God's perfect timing and his perfect answer.

My Heart's Cry to You, O Lord

Father, I admit that recent events have shaken me, and sometimes I feel as though my prayers will forever go unanswered. And yet, as soon as I begin to entertain this doubt, I know it's not true. I must put the full weight of my trust in your timing and your answers. Lord, help me to keep pressing forward in prayer and not become distracted by self-doubt or discouragement. Remind me to pray your powerful promises out loud as a reminder to myself of your wonderful, faithful care for us. I cannot change the outcomes, I know, but I can pray with persistence. Amen.

Finding Joyful Freedom in Self-Forgetfulness

1. Self-forgetfulness with others. "Let us throw off everything that hinders and the sin that so easily entangles." As I spend time in prayer this week interceding on behalf of others, I will be careful to not become discouraged or doubtful about God's willingness and ability to answer my prayers. I won't stop praying, even when those I'm praying for seem to run farther from God than ever before. Instead, I'll invest even more time to pray for each of them.

2. Self-forgetfulness in me. "Let us run with perseverance the race marked out for us, fixing our eyes on Jesus." Knowing that prayer involves spiritual warfare, I'll keep in mind that Satan would love nothing better than for me to grow discouraged and stop praying. Despite any temporary feelings of discouragement or doubt about the efficacy of prayer, by God's grace I will continue to intercede on behalf of those God places on my heart and mind.

3. Self-forgetfulness with God. "Consider him who endured such opposition from sinners, so that you will not grow weary and lose heart." Each evening this week, I'll read from the Gospels about Jesus' death and resurrection. I'll spend time meditating on Jesus' perfect sacrifice on the cross and how important it is that I never give up or grow weary interceding on behalf of others.

Chapter 23

Praying with Self-Forgetfulness for Eternal Purposes

For this reason I kneel before the Father, from whom every family in heaven and on earth derives its name. I pray that out of his glorious riches he may strengthen you with power through his Spirit in your inner being, so that Christ may dwell in your hearts through faith. And I pray that you, being rooted and established in love, may have power, together with all the Lord's holy people.

Ephesians 3:14–18

Grant me to rest on thy power and faithfulness, and to know that there are two things worth living for: to further thy cause in the world, and to do good to the souls and bodies of men; This is my ministry, my life, my prayer, my end. Grant me grace that I shall not fail.

Puritan Prayer

Gary, a retired veterinarian and widower with three sons and ten grandchildren, had laser-sharp spiritual focus. Though none of his sons and their families lived near him, he excelled at keeping in close contact with them. Why?

For many reasons—but none more important to Gary than that he prayed fervently and diligently for each of his family members. He believed with his whole heart that prayer has eternal consequences, and that interceding daily on behalf of his sons and their families would make all the difference in their journeys toward being more like Jesus.

Every morning during the work week, Gary called each of his sons at an established time for a quick ten-minute phone conversation. Although the script rarely varied, his sons looked forward to these brief minutes on the phone, chatting with their wise and loving father. Pen in hand, Gary always asked his sons three questions: What challenges do you face today? What cares or concerns do you have for your family? What are you most grateful for today?

These question-and-answer sessions kept them constantly in touch with one another. It was sort of like a round robin conversation—except that the sharing of these prayers and requests set off an explosion of intercession directly to God's throne, where Jesus lives to intercede for believers. Gary established this daily phone schedule soon after his wife of fifty years passed away. Before her death, Evelyn had been the primary conductor of prayer requests from the children to Gary. But when that changed, Gary quickly realized that if he didn't step up and assume the responsibility himself, the family prayer chain would be broken.

With each and every telephone conversation Gary initiated with his family, and eventually with friends and neighbors, he had eternal purposes in mind. A self-proclaimed introvert, Gary found it difficult at first to reach out and open up these conversations, even with his sons. But the Lord kept nudging him until he self-forgetfully set aside his naturally shy tendencies and took that faith-filled first step. Gary's sons and their families are eternally grateful that he did.

I loved hearing the story of this elderly Christian man who made it his life's mission to pray. I love that Gary was able to lean on the grace of God to help him overcome any personal limitations or discomfort so he could be present and available to intercede on behalf of his family, friends, and neighbors. Most of all, I loved hearing about his solid assurance that interceding on behalf of others has eternal repercussions.

If only each of us had a faithful spiritual mentor in our lives who would call (or email or text) us every morning for our most pressing prayer needs! If you don't have this person in your life, then why not be like Gary and take on this precious prayer mantle yourself? I wonder how God might change us through the process of praying for others. Would we grow in faith? Would we develop more robust prayer lives? Would we become more humble and grateful as we watched God answer our prayers? Would we grow closer to the heart of God because of the investment of time we chose to spend talking to our heavenly Father each day? Why not all of the above?

In my long years as a Christian, I've observed that the farther we remove ourselves from the world's noise, confusion, and distraction to purposefully spend time with God, the more we change—and over time, others might even notice that change in us. We will become more like our Lord and Savior Jesus Christ, and that is the best answer to any prayer.

Take-away Action Thought

I want my prayers to take on eternal purposes, so I will begin asking those I pray for eternally motivated questions. I will tailor my prayers for each person I intercede for, because I want God's best for each of them.

My Heart's Cry to You, O Lord

Father, my family and friends have so many urgent needs in their lives. Help me to pray for each of them consistently every day. As I intercede, please help me to better understand what their deepest needs might be, rather than being content to skim the surface of their lives with frivolous requests. Give me your divine wisdom and understanding as I talk with these dear ones. As I spend time in prayer interceding on their behalf, show me your heart on each and every issue. Holy Spirit, please guide my prayers. Jesus, hear my prayers. Father, may it please you to answer them according to your perfect will. Amen.

Finding Joyful Freedom in Self-Forgetfulness

1. Self-forgetfulness with others. "I pray that out of his glorious riches he may strengthen you with power through his Spirit in your inner being, so that Christ may dwell in your hearts through faith." This week I will intercede on behalf of everyone I know, that they will be strengthened with the power of the Holy Spirit in their inner beings so they can fulfill whatever tasks, responsibilities, and challenges await them.

2. Self-forgetfulness in me. "Together with all the Lord's holy people, to grasp how wide and long and high and deep is the love of Christ, and to know this love that surpasses knowledge." Each day this week, I will ask the Lord to reveal to me any areas of my life where I doubt the present and perfect love of God. I will ask the Lord to help me reframe any hardships or losses into one of eternal purposefulness.

3. Self-forgetfulness with God. "For this reason I kneel before the Father, from whom every family in heaven and on earth derives its name." In the morning when I wake up, I will kneel (literally or figuratively) before the Father and begin my day giving thanks for his past, present, and future faithfulness to me.

Chapter 24

How Self-Forgetfulness Changes the Way We View Our Weaknesses

His dominion is an eternal dominion; his kingdom endures from generation and generation. All the peoples of the earth are regarded as nothing. He does as he pleases with the powers of heaven and the peoples of the earth. No one can hold back his hand or say to him: "What have you done?"

Daniel 4:34–35

Anxiety is God-forgetting. It is the result of thinking that life is on your shoulders, that it is your job to figure it all out and keep things in order. . . . If you fall into this way of thinking, your life will be burdened with worry and your heart will be filled with dread. But there is a much better way. It is God-remembering. It rests in the relief that although it may not look like it, your life is under the careful control of One who defines wisdom, power, and love.

Paul David Tripp

W ithin the space of three days, I heard more dismal and dire diagnoses from my nearest and dearest than I had time to mentally unpack and absorb. One friend shared that her cancer had returned for a third time. Another friend asked me to pray for her daughter, who is fighting a life-threatening illness that has no cure. Then another friend called to ask for prayer for her grandchild, who needed a second surgery that would hopefully undo the damage done by an earlier surgical mistake.

On top of that, there's the small group of ladies with whom I meet every Wednesday. After we conclude our study, we go around the circle sharing praises and asking for prayer support. By the time we complete our circle, there's usually at least two pages of new requests to pray for during the upcoming week. While some requests are of the garden variety (needing a job, finding a new place to live, working through a difficult relationship, etc.), on this particular week, the majority of the prayer needs by far were of the frightening physical type.

Maybe it's just me, but when most of my friends and family are simultaneously dealing with scary diagnoses, it is exhausting to think about, live with, and pray for them. Aside from the obvious truth that the older we grow, the weaker our bodies become, I'm discovering that it's getting more challenging by the year to live in a state of continual joyous faith (see my book, *Joyous Faith: The Key to Aging with Resilience*) while struggling in an aging body. How does one embrace an attitude of intentional self-forgetfulness with regard to our physical weaknesses when our bodies loudly complain and distract us at every turn?

Personally, when my body hurts and my mind is racing because I don't feel well, I must accept that God has allowed this unwanted intersection of human weakness and life responsibility. How I choose to handle this lack of control will cause one of two responses. I will experience either anxiety because I'm

God-forgetting, or inner peace because I'm God-remembering. Yes, self-forgetfulness extends even into the corners of those challenges and difficulties we face in our human weakness.

It's true that anxiety is God-forgetting. And it's also true that peace is God-remembering. The harsh reality, from our human perspective, is that we are not in control. This truth hits us especially hard when our human weaknesses collide with our day-to-day responsibilities. We feel the angst of this collision in an especially painful way because our bodies remind us of our human frailty.

The bigger picture is this: God is always in sovereign control of what he allows (or restrains) from happening in our lives (and to our bodies). As Paul Tripp reminds us, "God-remembering rests in the belief that although it may not look like it, your life is under the careful control of One who defines wisdom, power, and love." And this passage from the book of Daniel emphasizes Tripp's statement: "He does as he pleases with the powers of heaven and the peoples of the earth."

This powerful biblical truth gives us peace beyond the reassurance we might get from any type of personal effort or plan. Knowing—really knowing in the deepest recesses of our hearts—that God is in absolute control of this world and everything that happens in it should enable us to exhale our fears, worries, and anxieties. Yet God knows our human frailties and our temptation to try and take control. If there is one area in life where intentional self-forgetfulness is especially difficult, it's this one.

May each of us lean hard into the faithful arms of Christ when our bodies are in pain, torn, and wretched. May we find in him our perfect peace. May we learn to be glad and rejoice that God does indeed do "what pleases him with the powers of heaven and the peoples of the earth."

Take-away Action Thought

When I feel undone by the physical weaknesses of myself or a loved one and become anxious because of the responsibilities before me, I will intentionally be a God-rememberer. I will not give way to fear and worry over a situation in which I have no control. Instead, I will open the Bible and read passages that speak about God's total sovereignty until I am at peace once more.

My Heart's Cry to You, O Lord

Father, I'm in that uncomfortable place again where I'm feeling physically weak and yet I'm reminded of all that I still need to accomplish. Please help me; please remind me that you are in absolute control of all that takes place in my life. Before this day even began, you already knew the challenges I would face. And knowing that, you have already provided the truth and comfort I need to get through this day. Help me to submit to your perfect plan. Help me to embrace an attitude of self-forgetfulness and focus on you alone. I am not in control, and I am grateful that you are. Please enable me to be a God-rememberer so that your precious peace guards my heart and mind this day. Amen.

Finding Joyful Freedom in Self-Forgetfulness

1. Self-forgetfulness with others. "He does as he pleases with the powers of heaven and the peoples of the earth." During this coming week, I will spend time praying for those I know are struggling with physical weakness or illness. I will look for encouraging Bible passages to share with these dear ones and remind them of God's promised faithfulness.

2. Self-forgetfulness in me. "His dominion is an eternal dominion; his kingdom endures from generation and generation." Every day this week, I will spend some time looking for specific Bible verses that describe God's sovereignty and power. I'll write out those that stand out as especially encouraging and powerful to me, so I'll have them ready the next time I'm feeling poorly and need a good word from God.

3. Self-forgetfulness with God. "No one can hold back his hand or say to him: 'What have you done?'" This week, I will begin a thankfulness diary. In this journal, I will write down what I'm thankful for. I'll include enough details along with the dates, so that in the coming months and years, I'll be able to specifically remember what God did on my behalf and for the good of those close to me.

Chapter 25

How Self-Forgetfulness Changes the Way We Think

God disciplines us for our good, in order that we may
share in his holiness. No discipline seems pleasant at
the time, but painful. Later on, however, it produces a
harvest of righteousness and peace for those who have
been trained by it. Therefore, strengthen your feeble
arms and weak knees. Make level paths for your feet, so
that the lame may not be disabled, but rather healed.

Hebrews 12:10–13

*God does not spare us from the ravages of disease, heartache,
and disappointment of this sin-cursed world. But God is
able to take all of these elements—the bad as well as the
good—and make full use of every one. God's infinite wisdom
then is displayed in bringing good out of evil, beauty out of
ashes. It is displayed in turning all the forces of evil that rage
against His children into good for them. But the good that
He brings about is often different from the good we envision.*

Jerry Bridges

O n her way to church for another meeting of the addiction recovery group she led, Caroline found herself humming the old hymn, "It Is Well with My Soul." Not blessed with a singing voice anyone other than God would appreciate, she joyfully hummed the chorus, sang the refrain, and then repeated the words, "It is well, it is well with my soul." Caroline believed those words right down to the deepest recesses of her soul.

"Thank you, Lord," she prayed, "for helping me get my head back on straight. This time last week, I didn't know if I would ever want to head back to this group. Too much sadness. Too much sorrow. Too many relapses. Too much regret. Too much of my overthinking and believing that when someone relapses, it's all my fault. Too much of us mere humans trying to force changes in the hearts of hurting folks who just aren't ready yet. Lord, help me to keep my eyes on you no matter what happens today. Help me to keep my thoughts on you alone. Amen!"

Caroline pulled into the church parking lot and grabbed her purse, Bible, and recovery bag full of resource materials, along with a container of freshly baked cookies. "Here we go, Lord. Let's go encourage one another this evening."

With determination written across her face and a renewed confidence in God alone, she entered the building and headed straight to the homey recreation room she helped design and decorate for recovery and inner healing. Cozy and inviting, it had comfortable seating with enough personal space for folks to feel connected but not closed in. And then there was the tantalizing smell of coffee, tea, and refreshments filling the air.

Taking a seat, she noticed she had thirty minutes before any early comers might meander through the door, so she opened her notebook and reviewed the notes and prayer requests she had written down from last week's group session. When Caroline got to Tina's name, she stopped and inhaled sharply. "Lord, you're going to have to help me share with the group about Tina's current condition. They need to know. We all need to pray for her."

Caroline looked up toward the ceiling and recalled that late-night call she'd received from her pastor, explaining that Tina had overdosed and was in the local hospital. No further information was available other than that Tina asked her group to pray for her—again.

"And we will, Lord. We will pray for her. My task tonight is to not allow Tina's relapse to cause others to give up on their own recovery journeys. I know how sneaky that stinking thinking is."

The discipline of the Lord is so much broader than the narrowly defined type of discipline that automatically comes to mind for most of us. Discipline isn't simply meting out punishment and issuing restrictions after someone does something wrong. Not in God's economy. God also uses the word *discipline* as a way to describe one of his many teaching methods. When we think of discipline, we need to learn to embrace the term rather than be repelled by it. God uses our weaknesses and failures to strengthen us, prepare us, and make us more able to serve.

Take Caroline's frustration and sadness when she heard about Tina's relapse and overdose. She immediately began replaying the evening's conversation at the recovery group. She wracked her brain for any clues from Tina that should have warned them of her state of mind. Caroline didn't recall any such warning signals.

Next, she blamed herself. Somehow, she should have known what Tina was going to do later that evening, right? After all, she was the designated leader of the recovery group.

Finally, Caroline realized what she was doing and how she had been wrongly assuming that she could control another's actions. She stopped herself short and prayed for the Lord to help her think biblically. Tina's actions were not Caroline's responsibilities. Tina was an adult who made her own choices. Caroline realized she had to push past the false guilt and take the courageous next step: being responsible, faith-filled, and self-forgetful. She slowly realized that though she could and did grieve for Tina, Tina's choices shouldn't hinder her from continuing to serve.

What would happen to pastors, teachers, and ministry leaders if they quit every time someone in their line of care made a mistake and walked away? There wouldn't be any pastors, teachers, or ministry leaders left. Wisely, Caroline brought her thinking around and reminded herself that any real change in people's lives is always in the hands of God. We can teach, mentor, encourage, and stand alongside others, but real changes occur only when the Holy Spirit begins a supernatural work in people's hearts. We have to get rid of our first impulse to embrace that "stinking thinking" that falsely concludes we might as well give up and walk away. God's discipline always begins with helping us to realign our thinking according to biblical truth. Lasting change starts from the inside out. Think about that!

Take-away Action Thought

When I feel like giving up because those I'm ministering to make poor choices, I will seek the wise counsel of a mature believer. I will prayerfully reframe the entire difficult situation from a biblical standpoint, knowing that God can take the very worst that happens and transform it into something eternally meaningful if I seek his wisdom and his will.

My Heart's Cry to You, O Lord

Father, this week has been one of the most painful in recent memory. When I agreed to serve in this leadership capacity, I never dreamed of how grief-stricken I would feel when someone relapsed and overdosed. Lord, I feel like I've failed this person in every way possible. And that feeling of guilt? Well, it makes me want to give up. But I know that you are able to take even the worst situations and transform them into something beautiful, something eternally meaningful. Please help me work through my feelings and stay on course. Help me to embrace whatever lesson you would have me learn so I'm better equipped if this ever happens again. Amen.

Finding Joyful Freedom in Self-forgetfulness

1. Self-forgetfulness with others. "No discipline seems pleasant at the time, but painful." Later on, however, it produces a harvest of righteousness and peace for those who have been trained by it. Each day this week, I will prayerfully choose one person to contact and offer a word of encouragement to their difficult situation. I'll be sure to share a precious portion of Scripture with them.

2. Self-forgetfulness in me. "Strengthen your feeble arms and weak knees. Make level paths for your feet, so that the lame may not be disabled, but rather healed." Each morning this week, I will begin my day with a prayer of thanksgiving to God and express to him my full confidence in the work he is doing in my life through the lifelong process of sanctification.

3. Self-forgetfulness with God. "God disciplines us for our good, in order that we may share in his holiness." I'll give thanks that I'm called one of his beloved children, and I will gladly submit to his discipline so I might be mature and complete. I'll take the time to write in my journal about any difficult events from this week that God helped me to rethink, reframe, and revisit from his eternal perspective.

Chapter 26

How Self-Forgetfulness Changes the Way We Speak

We will no longer be infants, tossed back and forth by the
waves, and blown here and there by every wind of teaching
and by the cunning and craftiness of people in their deceitful
scheming. Instead, speaking the truth in love, we will grow
to become in every respect the mature body of him who is
the head, that is, Christ. From him the whole body, joined
and held together by every supporting ligament, grows
and builds itself up in love, as each part does its work.

Ephesians 4:14–16

*Examine the fruit of your communication and trace that fruit
back to root issues in the heart. Seek and grant forgiveness,
not just once but as a moment-by-moment pattern. Take
up with joy the wonderful commands and principles of
the Word. Look for opportunities to apply the new things
God is teaching you about his way of communication.
With joy speak words that have been chosen because they
are acceptable to the Lord and beneficial to others.*

Paul David Tripp

K enna had been dreading the morning of the fourteenth. It was the court-appointed date when she was scheduled to speak on behalf of her two nephews about her only sibling's parental neglect. Kenna had one sister, Kinsey, who married right out of high school, had two boys in two years, and was divorced before she turned twenty-one. Kenna, the older of the two, helped Kinsey as much as her sister allowed.

Kenna's twice-weekly visits to Kinsey's apartment left little to her imagination about how difficult mothering was for her. Her heart broke for her sister's plight as a single mom, and she stepped in to assist every chance she was given. But Kinsey didn't want Kenna to get too close. Kenna guessed she was embarrassed at the constant state of disarray of her apartment, the lack of regular meals, and the boys' unkempt appearances.

While Kenna was troubled by the outward signs that Kinsey wasn't able to take adequate care of her two young sons, it was an unplanned evening visit that really alerted her to the seriousness of Kinsey's neglect. One night, Kenna knocked on her door but no one answered. From the hallway, Kenna could hear the boys crying, so she kept knocking and began calling out for her sister. A neighbor from across the hall came out and informed Kenna that her sister often left the boys, both under three years old, alone for hours each evening. Kenna was horrified.

What should she do? She stood fixed to the spot as her sister's neighbor continued to describe the nightly crying and yelling that emerged from behind their apartment door. Just as Kenna was about to call emergency services, Kinsey appeared, stumbling down the hallway. When Kenna questioned Kinsey, her sister couldn't understand why Kenna was so upset.

That troubling conversation was the turning point in their sisterly relationship. Kenna tried to get her wayward sister to understand the risk she was putting her children in every time she left them alone, but Kinsey only made excuses. Kenna warned her that social services would get involved and the boys would be placed in foster care. Kinsey shrugged off the warning. Kenna offered to take the boys to her home until Kinsey was in a more stable place in her life, but she refused to even consider it. Finally, after exhausting every reasonable option and suggestion for caring for her nephews in a healthy and safe environment, Kenna realized she would have to contact children's services on behalf of her beloved nephews.

Kenna gave her sister every opportunity to accept help with parenting her boys. She also offered her sister solutions to managing her overwhelmed heart and mind. But Kinsey refused every one of Kenna's attempts to help. Eventually, Kenna found herself in the last position she ever wanted to be: an adversary of her only sibling. But Kenna knew she had to do what was right for her young and vulnerable nephews. She had to speak up on their behalf because they couldn't do it for themselves.

Although she realized her actions might very well permanently sever her relationship with her sister, she stood firm. And with a bold and self-forgetful decision, Kenna initiated a conversation to warn her of what seemed to be the necessary next step to protect the boys. She would never forget the look on her sister's face or her torrent of angry words. But God gave Kenna the courage and the grace to stay calm and speak directly yet compassionately to her troubled sister. Rather than allowing despair to color her words and actions, Kenna looked ahead to the future and believed that God might still grab hold of her sister's hardened heart and bring her to himself.

Take-away Action Thought

When I am placed into the difficult position of having to speak the truth in love, I will pray in advance about my sensitive conversation. I'll ask the Lord to prepare my heart and mind so I won't give way to anger or harsh words. I'll lean on the abiding strength of Jesus to give me the words to speak that will hopefully bring light to a dark situation.

My Heart's Cry to You, O Lord

Father, never in my wildest dreams did I imagine I'd be placed in such a heartbreaking battle with people I care about so much. This tragic situation hurts me in every way possible. Please help me to navigate these troubled waters with your courage, grace, and strength. I just want it all to go away. And, if I'm being honest, I dread having yet another confrontational conversation with my loved one. Please help me. Give me your wisdom and your words to pierce her hardened heart. And help my dear one to know how much I love her. Amen.

Finding Joyful Freedom in Self-Forgetfulness

1. Self-forgetfulness with others. "We will no longer be infants, tossed back and forth by the waves, and blown here and there by every wind of teaching and by the cunning and craftiness of people in their deceitful scheming." Each day this week, I will pray for those who are in troubling or difficult situations and ask the Lord how I might be of encouragement to them. I will

write down in detail what I believe their deepest needs are and pray accordingly.

2. Self-forgetfulness in me. "Speaking the truth in love, we will grow to become in every respect the mature body of him who is the head, that is, Christ." When I am placed in the difficult position of having to keep another person accountable, I will bathe the entire conversation in prayer before I meet with them. I'll enlist the support of other mature believers to pray that my conversation is God-honoring and of mutual benefit.

3. Self-forgetfulness with God. "From him the whole body, joined and held together by every supporting ligament, grows and builds itself up in love, as each part does its work." This week I'll spend time reading in the Bible about how God views the body of Christ—that is, the church. I'll look up passages that describe the body of Christ and how God designed it to hold and work together for the edification of us all.

Chapter 27

How Self-Forgetfulness Changes the Way We Listen

Even in darkness light dawns for the upright, for those who
are gracious and compassionate and righteous. . . . They
will have no fear of bad news; their hearts are steadfast,
trusting in the LORD. Their hearts are secure, they will have
no fear; in the end they will look in triumph on their foes.

Psalm 112:4, 7–8

*There is nothing that I can give another that I do not
need myself. I may have known the Lord for many years,
but I need his grace as much today as I did the first
moment I believed. If there is any truth, life, hope, grace,
and good in my life, it is because of his work. The only
thing I bring to the table is my weakness and my sin.*

Paul David Tripp

Logan was busy washing his car in the driveway when his
teenage daughter Leah came zipping down to the end of
the cul-de-sac. As she jerked to a stop in the driveway,
her tires left a streak of black on the cement—permanent proof

of her reckless driving. Logan felt his jaw clench in anger. *How many times have I warned her about driving too fast? This is the last time!* He winced when he heard the car door slam shut. *And she doesn't give any thought to the car either!*

"Hey Dad!" Leah greeted him cheerfully as she jogged away from him toward the house.

"Wait a minute. Come back here. We need to talk," Logan said with as much self-control as he could muster.

"I'm in a hurry," she answered. "I'll be late for work, Dad. Can it wait?" She seemed oblivious to her reckless driving mere minutes earlier.

Logan shook his head. "Leah, how many times have I warned you about driving down our street so fast? You know better. There are children running up and down the sidewalk and playing in the street. You could have hit one of them. And there's absolutely no good reason for you to tear into our driveway like that. Look at the tire tracks you left. Don't you see them?"

Father and daughter stood staring at each other. Leah knew from previous conversations that there was nothing she could say that would help soothe his anger, so she simply chose to remain silent. But her dad wasn't going to let it go. "Did you hear what I just said? Aren't you going to answer me?"

After a moment, she took a deep breath and said, "Dad, I'm sorry. I was wrong and it was foolish of me to drive so fast on our street. I won't do it again—please, Dad, let me finish. I can't apologize if you won't let me talk. Don't shut me down."

Logan took a step back and closed his mouth. *Is that what I do?* he wondered. *Shut people down while they're trying to explain themselves? Whoa. I need to learn to listen better.*

Self-forgetfulness does change the way I listen. It has to. Otherwise, we will all fall into the pattern of sharing our thoughts and emotions with little concern as to how it might affect other people. Communication done properly and effectively includes attentive listening and carefully chosen words. Effective, God-honoring interchange between two people occurs only when both participants are able and willing to truly hear what the other is saying and then respond in a humble and compassionate manner.

Logan's admonishment to his daughter Leah was spot on, but he could have done better. How? Leah explained it to him. Her dad was right in communicating to her about driving carelessly.

Once Logan was agitated, however, he rarely had enough inner calm to truly hear what his daughter would say in response. After his conversation with her that day, he realized for the first time that he hadn't been making an effort to really listen.

What exactly does it mean to listen in a humble, self-forgetful way? First, we must set aside any past conversations that might worsen our heightened emotions and sabotage the present moment. Next, we need to listen with the intent to understand the who, what, where, when, and why of the other person's perspective. Finally, with true humility, we must listen with empathy and compassion, knowing that we stand in need of God's grace, forgiveness, and instruction just as much as everyone around us.

We listen self-forgetfully when we desire the very best for the person with whom we are speaking. We understand that we are like them in our mutual need for God's rescuing grace every minute of every day. Logan, for his part, has just begun a wonderful journey toward applying that principle to himself.

Take-away Action Thought

When I feel upset, impatient, or angry at someone for their actions or their words, I won't react until my heightened emotions have calmed. I'll remove myself from the volatile situation and take a few minutes to ask God to set a seal over my mouth until I can speak lovingly for the purpose of the other person's edification. I will ask God to help me to truly listen to what the other person is saying.

My Heart's Cry to You, O Lord

Father, I tried so hard to contain my emotions today. And honestly, I did better than I have in previous conversations with this person! I was upset by her actions, and I wanted to convey how dangerous they were. In this, I believe I communicated in a way that honored you. But I realized today that I continue to struggle with being a good listener. I'm far too eager to reply to another's words with my own rebuttal, and I'm not always patient enough to hear them out. Help me to use more self-control and truly humble myself, so I can hear what is and isn't being said. I desire only the best for my loved one, and in order to demonstrate that love I need to listen to them with a heart full of compassion, grace, and humility. Amen.

Finding Joyful Freedom in Self-Forgetfulness

1. Self-forgetfulness with others. "They will have no fear of bad news; their hearts are steadfast, trusting in the LORD." Before bed this week, I will quickly review the conversations of the day. I'll especially take note of any conversations where I had the opportunity to bring encouragement, compassion, and fresh hope to those I was interacting with. If I failed to offer a faith-filled perspective today, I'll revisit the topic with these individuals tomorrow.

2. Self-forgetfulness in me. "Even in darkness light dawns for the upright, for those who are gracious and compassionate and righteous." My personal checklist for the week will include speaking and listening to communicate grace, compassion, and righteousness toward others. I will not give way to my own personal preferences or be selfishly protective.

3. Self-forgetfulness with God. "Their hearts are secure, they will have no fear; in the end they will look in triumph on their foes." Each morning this week, I'll spend time praying for God's wisdom, strength, and grace to both speak and listen well so that I am prepared to be self-forgetful on both fronts.

Chapter 28

How Self-Forgetfulness Changes the Way We See People

The LORD is my shepherd, I lack nothing. He makes me
lie down in green pastures, he leads me beside quiet
waters, he refreshes my soul. He guides me along the
right paths for his name's sake. Even though I walk
through the darkest valley, I will fear no evil, for you
are with me; your rod and your staff, they comfort me.

Psalm 23:1–4

*A life that pleases the Lord is never a smooth road. Our
Shepherd guides us along the right path—paths of
righteousness. That is true, but sadly, we often shake off His
guiding hands. His path might interest us for a while, but
then we allow sin to beckon us down a detour. . . . We are so
prone to wander—so inclined to leave His path and run away
from His lordship. But how gracious and patient he is with us!*

Joni Eareckson Tada

Renee stood at the pharmacy counter, waiting to pick up new prescriptions for her husband Will, which she hoped would help ease his daytime agitation and counter his nightly sleeplessness. Renee prayed it would be so. Ever since Will had suffered a stroke six months earlier, their lives had been upended. On most days, she inwardly despaired that they had lost the marital intimacy they once cherished.

Will's stroke not only affected his physical body, but it also dramatically altered his temperament and personality. Before the stroke robbed him of his robust and healthy active self, he was a gentle giant of a man. Always courteous and generous hearted, he was known as someone who looked out for the welfare of others as a matter of principle. Not anymore.

These days, Renee feels herself run into the ground both physically and emotionally trying to care for Will's many needs. At first, she hoped that with time some of his emotional rough edges might soften. But six months later, she had difficulty seeing any hope for lasting change in Will's once lovable personality. He was angry. He was impatient. He was unkind, and on some days, he was even cruel to her.

Realizing the challenge she was up against trying to lovingly and sacrificially care for Will, Renee made sure she stayed in contact with close friends who helped her care for herself as she served him. They also helped her change the way she was seeing her now-disabled husband. She admitted she had fallen into despair and self-pity over her painful situation. And understandably so! What Renee faced was difficult and challenging—and unless she found her daily, moment-by-moment strength and grace in the Lord's empowerment, the future seemed overwhelming at best and at worst, impossible to survive.

Enter her Christ-exalting friends who helped Renee reframe her situation into faith-filled, God-honoring possibilities.

Her dear friends not only stood by her and supported her both practically and emotionally, but they also kept directing her back to God's word and his promised faithfulness. And that made all the difference.

Self-forgetfulness changes the way I see people. When I'm intentional about seeing difficult-to-love people through the lens of eternity, everything changes. My attitude is different. My thoughts are different. My actions are different. When I choose to set aside my expectations and desires in favor of meeting another's needs, joyful inner freedom explodes.

Renee discovered the reality of the amazing biblical principle that it is indeed more blessed to give than to receive. When she found herself at a breaking point because of exhaustion and sadness over losing what had been the norm in her marriage, she was at a crossroads. She had to decide whether or not she would grieve what once was and by God's enabling grace embrace the present, or remain stagnant and emotionally immobile. Renee's friends helped her better understand her mixed emotions and make the only real choice for a Christ-follower.

Renee recommitted to keeping her eyes on God as she simultaneously recommitted to love and serve her husband despite his present unlovable personality. She asked God to help her see Will through the lens of eternity and to love him even if he was unable or unwilling to love her back. Joyful freedom—that's where Renee is living today. And she will tell you it's a far better place to live than in disappointment, despair, and regret.

Take-away Action Thought

When I am faced with a life-altering change of events, I will find my constancy, my strength, and my stability in God alone. I won't rely on my ever-shifting state of emotions that rise and fall by the hour. I'll also seek out faithful friends and ask them to keep me accountable as I trust in God's perfect provision.

My Heart's Cry to You, O Lord

Father, you know my heart and you understand better than anyone how I'm feeling these days. I'm filled with sadness and grief over what once was, and I'm dreading what may be my permanent new normal. I know that these changes aren't anyone's fault, but they are still so hard to accept! My heart hurts when I remember how things used to be before this painful event stole the best part of my life. Please help me to trust you to meet all my needs as I meet the many needs of my loved one. Give me a joyful heart even in the midst of these daily difficulties. I need your supernatural grace and strength as I've never needed it before. Amen.

Finding Joyful Freedom in Self-Forgetfulness

1. Self-forgetfulness with others. "Even though I walk through the darkest valley, I will fear no evil, for you are with me, your rod and your staff, they comfort me." Every morning this week, before I even get out of bed, I will spend a few minutes praying for the strength,

wisdom, and grace to fulfill all my responsibilities. I will thank God in advance for the supernatural provision he provides for me each and every hour of the day.

2. Self-forgetfulness in me. "He makes me lie down in green pastures, he leads me beside quiet waters, he refreshes my soul." Daily, I will find a quiet place to refresh my body, settle my emotions, and nourish my soul. I'll drink something refreshing, read an inspirational book, and open up God's word to the book of Psalms.

3. Self-forgetfulness with God. "The LORD is my shepherd, I lack nothing." At the end of the day, I will talk to the Lord about my day and pour my heart out before him. I won't hold back on what I'm feeling. Instead, I'll literally cry out to God and tell him of my struggles and my needs. Then I'll thank him by faith for his promised provision, and I'll go to sleep at peace, confident in his trustworthiness to care for me.

Chapter 29

How Self-Forgetfulness Changes the Way We Interpret the World

Finally, brothers and sisters, whatever is true, whatever is noble, whatever is right, whatever is pure, whatever is lovely, whatever is admirable—if anything is excellent or praiseworthy—think about such things. Whatever you have learned or received or heard from me, or seen in me—put it into practice. And the God of peace will be with you.

Philippians 4:8–9

What comes to mind when you hear the word practice? I think of practicing the piano and learning multiplication tables as a child, and of learning German verbs as an adult. When we practice, we do something over and over. Practice isn't fun. It's boring and it's hard work. But Paul instructs us to practice "these things." What things? Choosing to give our anxieties to God. Choosing to pray specifically. Choosing to be thankful. Choosing to dwell on the positive. We are to practice substituting prayer for worry, the positive for the negative—and the God of peace will be with us!

Linda Dillow

Nicki, a content editor for a large newspaper, had been wondering lately if it was time for her to end her career. Though she wasn't quite at the age at which she had planned to retire, she thought long and hard about whether she had it in her to work four more years. In the past, Nicki had loved her job. She found it intellectually stimulating, and it gratified her needs as a detail-oriented person. But over the past few years, all she read and proofread was bad news. It was a constant barrage of negativity that affected her attitude at the office and beyond.

Maybe it was a sign of the times. Or perhaps it was a sign that she was simply getting older. She wondered if she was losing her ability to distance herself from the constant stream of murder, bombings, and every sort of violence. By the end of the workday, Nicki often felt as though the weight of the world was on her shoulders. In a way, she was right. Because she spent eight hours a day poring over every word and making sure the facts and context were accurately presented, she felt the weight of the stories she read.

For the umpteenth time, she wondered what had changed. Was it her? Was it the world? What should she do? She left work one night in a particularly dismal mood and again prayed about the perpetual funk she found herself fighting against. "Lord, help me to understand what's going on with me. Why am I so discouraged and depressed every day?" As Nicki stopped at a red light on her way home, she spotted a brand-new billboard to her right. It read, "Choose your thoughts with care, your mind can only dwell on one thought at a time. You decide if it's positive or negative. You decide."

Nicki read and reread that billboard slogan. Then she smiled to herself. "Okay, Lord, I see what you did there. Message received loud and clear."

We must practice, as Nicki discovered, to take every thought captive to the obedience of Christ—from the moment we open our eyes in the morning to when we finally close them at night. And given the content of the news in our world today, aren't we all in a position like Nicki's? For this reason, Linda Dillow's formula for choosing our thoughts is so timely. We learn to practice by "choosing to give our anxieties to God. Choosing to pray specifically. Choosing to be thankful. Choosing to dwell on the positive."

Bad news. Dismal headlines. Scary reports. Evil doings (and evildoers). It all makes for an overwhelmed and discouraged heart. Unless, of course, we take the mandate found in Philippians 4:8–9 to heart and obey Paul's instructions. What a difference it would make in you and me, if we deliberately chose to think about "whatever is true, whatever is noble, whatever is right, whatever is pure, whatever is lovely, whatever is admirable—if anything is excellent or praiseworthy."

How might we view our world differently if we decided to be self-forgetful about the way all the bad news drags us down and instead began thinking, speaking, and acting on all the good that is here by God's common grace?

The natural world God created is replete with beauty, creativity, and a glory born of his power alone. How might we feel differently about that which frightens us in the world if we choose to place our focus upon the true, noble, right, pure, lovely, admirable, excellent, and praiseworthy qualities of God as our Father?

Like Nicki, we will never discover the joyful freedom of self-forgetfulness unless we are determined to trust and obey

God's directives on what we choose to think about. If you're anything like me, you too are in need of a mental break from the world's woes. And no one but our loving heavenly Father can bring the peace we so need. But we have a choice.

Take-away Action Thought

When I feel overwhelmed and discouraged by the news of the world, I will stop myself from lingering in that negative mental space. I will read Philippians 4:8–9 out loud, and then I'll start listing everything I can think of that's true, noble, right, pure, lovely, admirable, excellent, and praiseworthy.

My Heart's Cry to You, O Lord

Father, I'm struggling again today with all the upsetting news I keep hearing. It seems like there is nothing but negative news anymore. Please help me to push aside these terrible incidents for a time. Help me to discipline my thoughts and place my full attention on what is true, noble, right, pure, lovely, admirable, excellent, and praiseworthy. I desire to keep my heart and mind on you, Lord. And I need the peace that only you can give. Fill my mind with your precious promises and grant me a settled and restful spirit as I take comfort in your sovereignty and righteous ruling over this world. Amen.

Finding Joyful Freedom in Self-Forgetfulness

1. Self-forgetfulness with others. "Finally, brothers and sisters, whatever is true, whatever is noble, whatever is right, whatever is pure, whatever is lovely, whatever is admirable—if anything is excellent or praiseworthy—think about such things." This week, I will be purposeful about encouraging those I come into contact with to choose to think on the positive, not the negative, in their lives. I'll even help them dig for the positive if they're struggling to think of something for which to give thanks!

2. Self-forgetfulness in me. "Whatever you have learned or received or heard from me, or seen in me—put it into practice." Each day this week, I'll take some time to mentally revisit the conversations I've had and the thoughts I'm entertaining. I'll ask myself if I'm choosing that which is praiseworthy to focus on or not. I will write out this Philippians 4 portion of Scripture and carry it with me for review as needed.

3. Self-forgetfulness with God. "The God of peace will be with you." Every evening, I'll spend a few minutes looking up verses that have the word *peace* in them. I will read carefully and consider all the wonderful implications of having the peace of God within me.

Chapter 30

How Self-Forgetfulness Changes the Way We Worship God

"Yet a time is coming and has now come when the
true worshipers will worship the Father in the Spirit
and in truth, for they are the kind of worshipers
the Father seeks. God is spirit, and his worshipers
must worship in the Spirit and in truth."

John 4:23–24

"The Valley of Vision"

Lord, high and holy, meek and lowly,
Thou hast brought me to the valley of vision,
      where I live in the depths but see thee in the
            heights;
      hemmed in by mountains of sin I behold thy glory.

Let me learn by paradox
      that the way down is the way up,
      that to be low is to be high,
      that the broken heart is the healed heart,
      that the contrite spirit is the rejoicing spirit,
      that the repenting soul is the victorious soul,
      that to have nothing is to possess all,

that to bear the cross is to wear the crown,
that to give is to receive,
that the valley is the place of vision.
Lord, in the daytime stars can be seen from
deepest wells,
and the deeper the wells the brighter thy
stars shine.
Let me find thy light in my darkness,
thy life in my death,
thy joy in my sorrow,
thy grace in my sin,
thy riches in my poverty
thy glory in my valley.

Puritan Prayer

Recently, I found myself standing in church next to my husband, my middle daughter and her husband, and our youngest daughter. As we were praising the Lord through song, I couldn't help but notice how deeply affected both of my daughters were by the lyrics of the hymn "How Great Thou Art," and it made my heart as a mother so thankful. Because I knew the unique challenges each of my daughters were facing in their lives, I realized they were both singing the lyrics while taking comfort in the greatness of our God.

It was a moment of pure and holy worship. I thanked the Lord again and again that my motherly prayers had been answered on so many occasions through the years as I interceded on behalf of all my four children. I remembered both the bitter and the sweet life events that had brought us all to our knees in prayer. Sometimes it was to cry out for help from God, knowing he was the only one who could rescue us. Other times, it was to rejoice in thanksgiving for God's blessed provision. And now, I was witnessing the fruits of those prayers in the lives of my daughters as I watched them self-forgetfully put aside the challenges that weighed on them in order to be fully present to worship and be renewed by God. Though they had big things to worry about in life at that time, they found peace when they—at least temporarily—set down those burdens to sing about God's greatness.

As I too worshipped the Lord that Sunday morning, I thought about the spiritual paradoxes found in life. The Puritan prayer above describes it best here: "Let me learn by paradox that the way down is the way up, that to be low is to be high, that the broken heart is the healed heart, that the contrite spirit is the rejoicing spirit, that the repenting soul is the victorious soul, that to have nothing is to possess all, that to bear the cross is to wear the crown, that to give is to receive, that the valley is the place of vision."

Self-forgetfulness changes the way I worship God. How can it not? Because God desires his children to worship him in spirit and in truth, we are called to look beyond our relationship challenges, financial status, health, or whatever else is worrying us, and place our hearts and minds on who God is.

God knows what challenges we will face in each moment. He knows that as we self-forgetfully lay these burdens aside so we can focus on gratefully worshiping him in spite of the difficulties in our lives, we will discover joyful freedom. And we will.

Like so many spiritual paradoxes found throughout Scripture, God asks us to trust and obey. We won't always understand,

and that's okay. We won't always like what God is allowing, but that's okay. We need to remember, however, that God is God and we are not! The more we intentionally elevate God through righteous biblical thinking that brings him honor and glory, the more clearly we see life through an eternal lens.

As we practice worshipping God in spirit and in truth no matter what we face today, the supernatural paradox that changes us from the inside out begins. We trust God. We obey God. We are then able to spill out worship to him even when our hearts are breaking and our strength is waning. And once we give from the deepest part of ourselves, God is pleased and joyful freedom calms our hearts.

 Take-away Action Thought

When life is getting me down, I will purposefully set aside all of my woes and troubles, and I will worship and praise the Lord. In spite of my personal struggles, I will quiet my heart and mind and sing to him about all the glory that is due to him.

My Heart's Cry to You, O Lord

Father, these obstacles feel so overwhelming to me. I don't see any way around these difficulties, so I must go through them. Please help me to trust you to give me exactly what I need to endure. Help me to keep my heart and mind focused on you and your promised provision. I know I'm not strong enough, not resilient enough, not wise enough to traverse this season alone. I want to worship you in spirit and truth. Give me the grace to honor you by trusting you in my heart and with my voice. Amen.

Finding Joyful Freedom in Self-forgetfulness

1. Self-forgetfulness with others. "Yet a time is coming and has now come when the true worshipers will worship the Father in the Spirit and in truth." Each evening this week, I will pray for my closest family members and friends and ask the Lord to give each of them the grace to set aside whatever it is they are struggling with so they can worship him fully and exalt his name no matter what circumstances they are facing.

2. Self-forgetfulness in me. "They are the kind of worshipers the Father seeks." During my quiet times, I will prayerfully offer up my worship to God in words and song. I'll pay close attention to the lyrics of the worship music I sing so that both my heart and mind are enriched through theologically rich hymns and songs.

3. Self-forgetfulness with God. "God is spirit, and his worshipers must worship in the Spirit and in truth." This week, I will spend time searching the Scriptures for verses that speak of worshiping in spirit and truth so I can develop a better and deeper understanding of this essential Christian discipline.

Sources for Quotations

1. Linda Dillow, *Calm My Anxious Heart* (Colorado Springs: NavPress, 2007), 35.

2. Edward Welch, *A Small Book for the Anxious Heart* (Greensboro: New Growth Press, 2019), 104.

3. Welch, *Anxious Heart*, 64.

4. Paul David Tripp, *New Morning Mercies* (Wheaton: Crossway, 2014), January 14 entry.

5. Paul David Tripp, *Instruments in the Redeemer's Hands* (Phillipsburg, NJ: P& R, 2002), 84.

6. Edward Welch, *A Small Book about a Big Problem* (Greensboro: New Growth Press, 2017), 135.

7. Linda Dillow, *A Deeper Kind of Calm* (Colorado Springs: NavPress, 2006), 47.

8. Andrew Murray, *Humility* (Minneapolis: Bethany House, 2001), 57–58.

9. Jerry Bridges, *Trusting God* (Colorado Springs: NavPress, 1988), 52.

10. Tripp, *New Morning Mercies*, February 1 entry.

11. Tim Lane and Paul Tripp, *Relationships: A Mess Worth Making* (Greensboro: New Growth Press, 2006), 135–36.

12. Welch, *Big Problem*, 158–59.

13. Paul David Tripp, *War of Words* (Phillipsburg, NJ: P&R, 2000), 39.

14. Tripp, *New Morning Mercies*, February 16 entry.

15. Nancy Leigh DeMoss, *Choosing Gratitude* (Chicago: Moody, 2009), 113–14.

16. Welch, *Big Problem*, 99.

17. Oswald Chambers, *My Utmost for His Highest* (Grand Rapids: Discovery House), March 14 entry.

18. Chambers, *My Utmost for His Highest*, February 23 entry.

19. Arthur Bennett, ed., *The Valley of Vision: A Collection of Puritan Prayers and Devotions* (Carlisle: The Banner of Truth Trust, 2007), 334–35.

20. Tripp, *New Morning Mercies*, February 26 entry.

21. Welch, *Anxious Heart*, 19–20.

22. Bridges, *Trusting God*, 185.

23. Bennett, ed., *The Valley of Vision*, 343.

24. Tripp, *New Morning Mercies*, March 13 entry.

25. Bridges, *Trusting God*, 119–20.

26. Tripp, *War of Words*, 133.

27. Tripp, *War of Words*, 149–50.

28. Joni Eareckson Tada, *A Spectacle of Glory* (Grand Rapids: Zondervan, 2016), 153.

29. Dillow, *Calm My Anxious Heart*, 33.

30. Bennett, ed., *The Valley of Vision*, xxiv–xxv.